The Problem-Solving Handbook
for High School Journalism Advisers

by

Bruce L. Plopper, Ph.D.

Department of Journalism
University of Arkansas at Little Rock

Illustrated by Amy Ness

Published by
QUILL AND SCROLL FOUNDATION
School of Journalism and Mass Communication
The University of Iowa
Iowa City, Iowa 52242

Copyright 1992 by Bruce L. Plopper
and Quill and Scroll Foundation

Acknowledgments

This publication owes its existence to a variety of sources who contributed to it in many ways. The idea that high school journalism advisers needed assistance wouldn't have blossomed into a handbook had it not been for my wife's support, which continued unabated through the difficult and uninspired times I sometimes experienced during the writing process. This handbook is dedicated to her.

The high school journalism teachers who shared their problems and the solutions they devised for those problems also contributed to this handbook, for without their ideas, the wealth of information contained in the handbook would have been noticeably smaller.

Pam James and Melissa Wilson also made this a better handbook because they painstakingly read the manuscript for language errors and made numerous suggestions to improve its readability. Others who contributed by reviewing the handbook and offering suggestions included Mary Benedict, Professor Emeritus of Indiana University School of Journalism; Jack Dvorak, Indiana University School of Journalism; Thomas Eveslage, Temple University School of Journalism; Richard Johns, executive director of Quill and Scroll Society, University of Iowa; and James Whitfield, graduate student, University of Iowa.

Finally, the University Research Council of the University of Central Arkansas provided financial assistance over a two-year period to support the production of this handbook.

Preface

This handbook is a problem-solving guide for journalism teachers who advise student publications. It is neither a textbook for introductory journalism classes nor a student manual for high school publications.

It was created because no existing journalism text adequately discusses the day-to-day problems that most high school journalism advisers encounter. Published articles concerning high school journalism and discussions with high school journalism teachers throughout the United States indicate that these problems are nearly universal in this nation's high schools.

In short, the handbook addresses such problems in detail, offering guidance that has worked well in a variety of environments. It also contains lists of helpful sources and materials.

Section I offers solutions to the problems that advisers encounter when dealing with high school journalists. Section II confronts performance problems specific to the day-to-day job of high school journalism advisers. Section III addresses problems that administrators generate for high school journalism programs. Section IV provides suggestions for handling problems created by school and nonschool personnel not directly involved in the publication program, and problems associated with other aspects of the operation. The final section is a guide to resources for journalism advisers.

Ideally, this handbook will be an immediate aid for currently employed high school journalism teachers and a supplementary college text in courses designed to train high school journalism teachers.

--Bruce L. Plopper

Iowa City, Iowa
May 1992

Contents

Acknowledgments iii
Preface iv
Introduction - What It Means to be A Journalism Teacher 1

Section I - Solving Problems Associated with Students 3

1. Increasing Motivation and Enthusiasm 4
2. Helping Students to Take Journalism Seriously 7
3. Overcoming Irresponsibility 9
4. Enhancing Poor Skills 11
5. Combatting Unrealistic Expectations 16
6. Making the Most of Dysfunctional Staff Members 18
7. Coping With Personal Conflict, Jealously, and Self-Interest 20
8. Teaching Students to Accept Criticism 23
9. Preparing for Personnel Changes 24

Section II - Solving Problems Associated with Advisers 27

10. Sustaining Motivation and Enthusiasm 28
11. Building Experience and Knowledge 30
12. Expanding Instruction Time 32
13. Selecting Staff Members the Right Way 35
14. Overcoming Problems Generated by Predecessors 37
15. Providing and Accepting Criticism Gracefully 39
16. Avoiding Taking Over 41
17. Grading Guidelines Made Reasonable 43
18. Retracing Old Ground the Painless Way 45

Section III - Solving Problems Associated with Administrators 47

19. Building Support, Understanding, and Expectations 48
20. Beating the Budget Blues 50
21. Maximizing Class Scheduling and Classroom Assignments 53
22. Looking Forward to Bidding the Publication 56
23. Meeting Censorship Wisely 58
24. Resolving Requests for Favors 61
25. Handling Personnel Changes 63

Section IV - Solving Other Problems 65

26. Clarifying Adviser/Journalist Roles 66
27. Encouraging Students Not Involved in Journalism 68
28. Training Colleagues, Substitute Teachers, Parents, and News Sources to be Your Allies 70
29. Motivating Community Business Owners and Managers 73
30. Keeping Outside Production Personnel at Their Best 75
31. Dealing with Natural Disasters and Human-Produced Disasters 78
32. Adding Computers to Your Program 80
33. Distributing the Publication 82

A Final Note -- What You Can Do to Help 84

Section V - Guides to Resources 85

Organizations Relevant to High School Journalism 86
Publications Useful to High School Journalism Advisers 88
Companies Offering High School Journalism Production Aids 91

Introduction
What It Means to be A Journalism Teacher

Journalism teachers may play the most important roles of all in transmitting the American heritage of freedom to new generations, for teaching journalism, in the truest sense, means teaching students what it means to be at the heart of society's information exchange. To do this effectively, journalism teachers must teach their students a general knowledge of journalism history, an understanding of the journalistic process, and an appreciation of the freedoms and responsibilities inherent in the profession.

Now let's face it. That's a lot to ask of any high school journalism teacher. In fact, because high school journalism sometimes is a subject taught by the most available teacher, it's a wonder that some teachers achieve even one of the goals listed above. Such situations exist because some states require little undergraduate training in journalism in order to teach it; however, some teachers realize that they are ill-prepared.

Most likely, you wouldn't be reading this material if you felt completely prepared to teach journalism and to advise the high school publication that probably is associated with your class; it's to your credit that you want to prepare yourself more fully for journalism teaching and advising. Although this handbook may not be the definitive work concerning journalism teaching, it is an aid that will make your life easier. In fact, you might think of its contents as advice from a concerned ally who is interested in your welfare and the welfare of high school journalism in general.

As a high school journalism teacher, your life is difficult because you have few highly motivated students, because the students you do have are not terribly well-versed in English language usage, and because your students have little or no formal training or experience in journalism. In short, they watch television. This is unfortunate because from television they learn that journalism is generally superficial and often entertaining. What they do not learn from television is that journalism is one of the major elements in our society that holds our social structure together, thereby playing a very significant role in our culture.

In addition, your life will be made difficult by administrators, colleagues, parents, students not enrolled in your journalism class, and members of the community who do not realize how much you and your students have to do, how complicated a process it is, and how little time there is to do it.

So what does this have to do with your role as a journalism teacher? Put quite simply, it is your responsibility, against extreme odds, to show your students how important journalism is to our society, to help them perceive journalism as a serious endeavor, and to guide them as they encounter the normal problems associated with high school journalism.

To achieve your potential for making journalism a meaningful part of your students' lives, you must be a better-than-average teacher. This means that you must know your subject matter exceptionally well, maintain unlimited enthusiasm for your material, and meet all relevant problems with the attitude that they can be solved. These are universal characteristics of great teachers.

It is not easy to attain this Renaissance ideal, but it's not impossible. Teachers who were journalism majors have an advantage, while teachers who receive journalism assignments either because they have completed relevant coursework (perhaps even a journalism minor) or because they have expressed an interest in journalism will have a more difficult time. In states that do not require university coursework in journalism as a prerequisite to teaching it, teachers also may receive journalism assignments by default (either they are the newest teachers in the system or it is "their turn" to teach the course). Certainly, teachers in this position have the most disadvantages.

By whatever path you traveled on your way to becoming a journalism teacher, you will find that once you have arrived, it will be to your advantage to communicate, to anyone who will listen, the value of journalistic training for "life" activities. These are the pleasures and the tasks that all of us, no matter what our occupations, are engaged in at one time or another. For example, your serious journalism students will gain the following:

1) an appreciation for local, regional, national, and world news, which helps us to understand our environment;

2) an ability to analyze issues and synthesize points of view, which helps decision-making in all aspects of life;

3) a skill for oral and written communication, which enhances the ability to function in nearly every occupation;

4) a sense of responsibility that encourages regular work habits and persistence to complete tasks, which is generally necessary for personal and professional success;

5) a sense of journalism that promotes higher expectations and better evaluations of journalism at all levels of society.

Of course, if your students are members of a publication staff, they also will gain a variety of interpersonal skills and production skills that are invaluable in a variety of business and social situations.

The reason you will want to communicate this information to administrators, guidance counselors, colleagues, parents, and students is that it will help them all to form more serious opinions of your journalism classes. In turn, in the long run, you will be a less frustrated journalism teacher.

In summary, high school journalism teachers have several very important responsibilities to their students, and they face a variety of problems that are unique to the journalism subject area. No teacher is able to prevent or solve all of the problems, all of the time. During the school year, they also experience perhaps more mental anguish than other teachers, but the problems that cause their anguish provide them with the opportunity to evolve as teachers. The ideas and suggestions in this handbook will help you to nurture the personal growth and fulfill the responsibilities that define what it means to be a journalism teacher.

SECTION I

SOLVING PROBLEMS ASSOCIATED WITH STUDENTS

CHAPTER 1

Increasing Motivation and Enthusiasm

To address the lack of motivation and enthusiasm some students show toward journalism, the problem may be divided into several related areas. Not only is there a problem in recruiting enthusiastic and skilled students to serve on the publication staff, but there are similar problems concerning staff members' motivation to cover assignments, meet deadlines, engage in fund-raising activities, and promote the publication.

Obtaining Talented Staff Members

Although it is meaningless to rank order the motivational problems that advisers encounter, one such problem ranking near the top of all advisers' lists concerns the number and quality of students who sign up or volunteer to be staff members. The question becomes, "How do advisers motivate a reasonable number of talented students to become staff members?"

The answers vary, but there are several techniques you can use to ensure that at least some desirable students join your staff. One method involves active recruitment. Cultivate "bright" students in your other classes, and guide them toward the publication. Also, seek information from trustworthy students and other teachers; ask them to recommend students whom they think are highly motivated and talented in areas useful to you. Honors English classes often are good places to start your search for good writers, and photography classes, if your school offers them, are good places to recruit staff photographers.

Another technique involves efforts to convince talented staffers to remain on staff from one year to the next. In-staff training programs, through which freshmen, sophomores, and juniors are groomed for future editorial board positions, often serve this purpose.

To ensure that you obtain qualified students from the ones who express an interest in becoming staff members, be certain to insist that all potential staff members fill out applications. These should require them to designate why they want to become staff members and what they plan to do as staff members. Many advisers also give skills tests that involve spelling, grammar, writing, and editing exercises. Others check applicants' gradepoint averages and other commitments (involvement in other activities can dramatically cut down time devoted to student publications), obtain samples of applicants' written or photographic work, and seek relevant information from other teachers and students who know the applicants fairly well.

Covering Assignments and Meeting Deadlines

Once you have been able to secure a core group of motivated and talented editors and reporters, you face another problem: how do you guarantee that your entire staff will be motivated and enthusiastic about covering their assignments and meeting deadlines?

Part of the solution to this problem is generated at the very beginning of the term, in your initial address to the staff. It concerns the attitude that your staff has about journalism, and more specifically, their attitude toward their publication. When you begin the term, you need to make it clear that producing the student newspaper or yearbook is really journalism, and that it must be taken seriously. Tell your students about the importance of journalism to society and that you expect a lot from them as journalists. You might survey your staff about their journalistic beliefs and about their beliefs concerning their publication, all the while aiming for consensus that their endeavor is really important.

In addition to displaying your own enthusiasm and motivation toward journalism, you may motivate your students by asking media professionals and university professors to address your class. If you coach them, they will make every effort to come to your aid by conveying the message of media's importance and the seriousness of the task at hand. Your efforts, coupled with the efforts of guest speakers, act to instill pride in your students concerning their work.

Of course, if you plan to enter your students' work in scholastic journalism contests, let your students know this at the beginning of the year. This also provides an opportunity to discuss the importance of the team approach to journalism. While your students may be vying for individual honors, they also must be concerned with the overall effort, which requires teamwork akin to any sport your school plays.

In convincing your students to cover their assignments and meet their deadlines, it is often useful to discuss with them the process of journalism.

This involves noting that there is some natural tedium and boredom associated with journalism, but that it comes with the territory and should not be an excuse for not doing what needs to be done. To counteract the tedium and boredom, you might allow staff members to choose their own assignments as often as possible, and you might recognize student achievements as often as possible. You might even establish individual periodic awards, such as "the most helpful staffer" award and "the sore thumb" award, which recognize achievement and dysfunction, on a regular basis (weekly or monthly).

If there are certain areas that no one volunteers to cover, you might institute a "beat" system similar to those used by professional newspapers. For example, one student could be responsible for news from the principal, one could report on developments associated with student government, and one could cover club news. Assigning specific students to specific beats helps to instill responsibility in your reporters, for they are expected to cover these beats for a given time period. The more experience your staffers have with given beats, the more familiar they become with the topics and the better work they do.

To help your students meet deadlines, you must explain to them the consequences of missing one. Tell them they are links in a production chain that relies upon timing, and that if one link breaks, the work of all the other links is disrupted. Explain that typesetting businesses and printing businesses are tightly scheduled, and if their customers do not meet mutually agreed upon schedules, the customers must suffer the consequences, e.g., not receiving the finished product on time. Even if your publication is merely typed and photocopied, reporting delays will cause publication delays.

You might take this line of thinking one step further by explaining that production delays can cause vast embarrassment if announcements and advertisements that are deadline related do not reach their intended audiences in time for the deadlines to be met, e.g., club meetings or company sales tied to time limits.

You also might add some peer pressure in order to motivate your students to meet their deadlines. For example, if your school has daily announcements that are read either over a public address system or by teachers in first period classes, create an announcement that indicates the date your publication will be available. This creates anticipation on the part of students not enrolled in your class, and in turn, peer pressure from outside. In order to create peer pressure from within, you can tell your staff members that if they meet their deadlines, you will reward them with free time, bonus points toward their grades, staff parties, or field trips. Of course, your rewards will depend upon your teaching environment and your budget.

When your students are chronically unresponsive to deadline pressures, you will find false deadlines very useful. This means that you designate deadlines that fall in advance of actual deadline dates (by as much as a week or two, depending on your publication schedule). This allows your students to actually miss a deadline, without too much consequence. Be aware, however, that students will soon catch on to the false deadline scenario if you use it frequently.

A technique similar to the false deadline method involves the use of "lost days," which protects you and your students from unplanned loss of time. This idea may be used in your own teaching schedule to compensate for loss of class time due to school closings, unscheduled assemblies, and other unforeseen reasons for not completing your lesson plans. It may be used by your staff members to compensate for time lost due to similar obstacles. To use the "lost days" technique, people in charge of scheduling deadlines decide exactly how much time it should take to complete the material during a given deadline period, and then they automatically add a few days to each deadline period. As deadline periods increase in length, larger numbers of "lost days" are added.

Certainly, as an aid in meeting deadlines of any kind, poster-size calendars should be placed in high visibility areas within the classroom. These calendars should include descriptions of the materials needed for each deadline, the names of students responsible for the materials, and spaces to indicate exactly when the materials have been gathered.

Raising Funds

Concerning your students' lack of enthusiasm for participating in fund raising for the publication, a variety of solutions may be pursued. At the outset, you must be enthusiastic about it and you must make every effort to make it fun.

Beyond that, as with the deadline problem, you can offer rewards on both individual and group bases. Such rewards can take the form of cash incentives (commissions), other goodies (staff parties), free ad space in the publication, or, in the case of the yearbook staff, a free yearbook. You can create the kind of reward schedule that fits your situation, in terms of finances, time, and space.

One aspect of fund raising that many advisers overlook is that their students do not know how to sell advertising. At the beginning of the year, you need to set aside some time to discuss with your students the techniques of selling. If you are not adequately trained to do this, you might ask a sales representative you know to give a presentation on the art of selling.

Furthermore, at first, you might send your students to sell advertising in pairs. This helps to build their confidence and to overcome the shyness some of them might have toward approaching people they do not know.

After most of your students have attempted to sell ads (maybe even after the first full-blown sales day), hold another group discussion and find out what worked and what didn't. This sharing of information can be very comforting and encouraging to those involved.

You'll also want to suggest to your students that they seek out companies which either have not advertised with you previously or which do business with your school. Both are likely targets for sales. Often, new advertisers can be enticed by creating mock-ups of advertisements containing pictures of their businesses. Another technique that works well involves the use of holiday-related ads, which may bring more new advertisers to your publication.

Regardless of the size of your staff, if there is a business or marketing club at your school, you might suggest to the club's sponsor that members could earn money (commissions) and gain relevant experience by selling ads for the school's publications. Often, these club members are so motivated that your students won't have to engage in what they may consider to be nonjournalistic activities.

To sell an increased number of annuals and newspaper subscriptions, you might also initiate discounts for first-day orders. Not only will this procedure increase your overall sales, but it will provide your staff with a certain amount of operating revenue with which to begin the school year.

In terms of pure fund-raising activities, you might sell certain items on a regular basis (e.g., candy, gum, nuts, balloons, or buttons), to support the publication. Some schools even have concession stands run by student clubs. Talk to local vendors about pursuing such projects, which might be similar to those currently used by other organizations in your school or community. Also, to raise funds for their publication, your students might agree to perform group services such as carwashing, lawnmowing, or snow shoveling.

Finally, as a means of encouraging your students in their sales endeavors, create charts and posters to show the progress of the group as a whole and of individuals in particular. These charts should contain indications of the goals you hope to reach as well as landmarks along the way.

Promoting the Publication

Another problem relating to student motivation and enthusiasm concerns promotion of the publication. Often, students who engage in editorial or production activities do not wish to spend additional time selling and distributing the publication. If you have a large enough class or staff, you may create a special task force to sell and distribute your newspaper or yearbook, but you need to be sure these students also fulfill other responsibilities. They may not be your writers, editors, and photographers, but they must perform some other function because sales and distribution will not take up enough of their time in a classroom situation. You can require them to submit a minimal number of items for publication, no matter how competent they are as writers, for even if their work is not publishable, the stories they have uncovered may be worth pursuing.

If you do not have the luxury of a large staff, you need to make clear at the beginning of the year that everyone must take part in sales and distribution, and you can set goals for each student and create posted schedules pertaining to sales deadlines and distribution activities.

To overcome lagging sales, ask your students to dis-

cuss their publication whenever they meet with other clubs or organizations to which they belong. Also, in all mailings sent to parents, and at all school assemblies, make announcements about the publication. This will keep the publication in the public eye.

As mentioned above, there are many ways to combat students' lack of motivation and enthusiasm, as applied to student publications. There is no need to spend time in the teachers' lounge complaining about this problem; take these suggested solutions, expand upon them, and do something about the problem. Your life will be more fun if you do.

CHAPTER 2
Helping Students to Take Journalism Seriously

A teacher fosters a lot of impressions at the beginning of every new class, directly and indirectly, through verbalizations, actions, and overall demeanor. Even in a school where a teacher has a positive reputation based on past behavior, that instructor has the opportunity to forge new class expectations at the outset of each school year.

To prevent a year-long battle with students who think journalism is like a school club, at the beginning of the semester, you must convince the students that journalism should be taken seriously. This is primarily done by showing that you do not consider it to be a frivolous way to spend time.

If you do not convince students that you take journalism seriously, then your students will not take journalism seriously either. Remember, you are the most visible example of how journalism should be approached. If the students get the wrong idea to begin with, then these students will neglect their assignments, and they will put only a minimal amount of effort into other important tasks.

Additionally, for students in charge of a publication to take their work seriously, you must convince them that it is their publication, and that you are the adviser, not a staff member. Don't end up typing articles and doing a majority of the work for the students. Teach them that the publication is their responsibility, and that you will not save the day for them when deadlines approach.

While the problem of "taking over" is fully discussed in Chapter 16, it should be noted here that when you do your students' work for them, as innocent as it may seem, you are saying to them, "Don't take journalism seriously. It's okay to ignore deadlines. Someone will always be there to pick up where you leave off." In journalism, as in life, this does not happen. Possibly by missing a deadline, you can show students the consequences of such a costly mistake. Experience can be the best teacher, so don't take too much responsibility onto yourself. Put the responsibility where it belongs, on the shoulders of the students.

In addition to setting the tone of seriousness about journalism and your role as an adviser, you will often have to clarify students' vague notions about journalism in general and teach them from scratch about the procedures involved in producing a publication. Thus you might use the first few days of class to discuss the meaning and processes of journalism, while at the same time instilling in the students the serious outlook you want them to have toward their responsibilities.

The paragraphs below describe a variety of ways to use discussions of journalism to encourage serious journalistic attitudes. Certainly, you won't have time to use all of the approaches during the first few class periods, but many of them may be used throughout the school year. While you may find it necessary to create personalized variations on specific themes, in one way or another they all should be helpful.

Definition of Journalism

One appropriate way to begin is by asking the students to write down their definitions of journalism, which you could collect and read to the class. Then, after discussing several of these definitions, you might quote the definitions that some professional, well respected journalists have used to describe journalism and compare them with definitions the students have provided.

Another technique is to compare journalism to keeping a daily, weekly, or monthly journal in which details of events are recorded. When the students understand the definition of a journal, they might be able to understand how journalism is considered the work of collecting and writing for a journal.

To collect and write for a publication such as a high school newspaper or yearbook, journalism requires an awareness of what goes on in the school. You might also mention that, in a broader sense, it means being aware of what goes on in the community, the state, the country, the world, and the universe.

Essentially, when journalism students understand that they must continually be aware of their surroundings and that they must record the events which occur in these environments, it is easy for them to see how serious journalism is. They become more aware of the amount of work involved. They also become more aware of the importance of that work, as reflected by the purposes of journalism.

Purposes of Journalism

Another way to help students realize that they should take journalism seriously is to discuss its purposes. In a broad sense, journalism serves many purposes. We know, for example, that it serves as a record of newsworthy events (some say it is history written in a hurry), but we also know that it can be used to persuade and to entertain. The students may not realize how many purposes journalism serves, although they have lived with mass media all of their lives.

To introduce this subject to the students, you might want to divide the class into small groups and ask them to spend 10 minutes creating a list of all the purposes of journalism. When time is up, ask the designated group leaders to read their lists. The master list resulting from the students' brainstorming will also help the students realize what journalism is all about and how it works.

Another technique that emphasizes the importance and the effects of journalism as it is practiced at your school is to discuss with the students how their publications serve as written and pictorial histories of the school. No matter what the student newspaper publication schedule is, each edition is a record of events that occurred during the school year. The same is true for the yearbook, whether it is published in the spring or in the fall.

Student publications also are public relations devices for the school, in more ways than one. Not only do parents and other members of your community read the student newspaper and yearbook, but people in other school districts often form their opinions of the school by reading your school's publications. These are points that many student journalists do not realize, without the guidance of their adviser. So it is very important to point this out to the students at the beginning of the academic year and to restate this thinking throughout the year.

Additionally, you might explain to your students that the school's publications have the potential to set the behavioral tone for the student body. When students see that publication staff members take the school seriously, the students, in turn, may evolve into better school citizens. In the long run, the publications also may influence your school's administrators, both in terms of how they view your school's journalism program and in terms of how they view controversies that arise in your school. Be aware, however, that editorially, student publications have the potential to make favorable or unfavorable impressions which school administrators can and will remember for a long time. A poorly thought out editorial philosophy may eventually backfire and hurt your program.

Given these purposes, and a serious discussion of them, the students should begin to develop a serious attitude toward journalism. As an added guarantee that this occurs, you might also discuss the qualities that characterize a good journalist.

Definition of A Good Journalist

Students may think that as journalists they can write about anything in any way. For them to develop a more professional and serious outlook, you need to discuss with them the characteristics of a good journalist.

You will need to teach them that responsible reporting is an integral part of their freedom of the press. While they may have the freedom to write about nearly everything, they must temper this freedom with the knowledge that not everything is worth writing about and not everything should be written about. In other words, some topics are not newsworthy, while the newsworthiness of other topics is counterbalanced by legal and ethical considerations. A good journalist knows what is newsworthy, what isn't, and what should stay out of print.

An experienced journalist evaluates events in terms of many factors, including timeliness, impact on the audience, prominence of the people involved, amount of conflict or drama, human interest, and proximity, to name a few. Whether journalists are members of high school publications or major newspapers, they develop "a nose for news" that guides them in their quest for publishable information.

Tell the students that good journalists are aware, curious, and accurate, and discuss these three characteristics through illustrations. To develop awareness, encourage the students to use all of their senses and, like sponges, to absorb every detail of events about which they write.

Also tell them that the old axiom, "curiosity killed the cat," doesn't apply to journalism. The students need to ask questions and play the part of a young child who always ask "why?" Suggest that they also ask who, what, why, where, when, and how (the 5 w's and h). Emphasize to the students that the only dumb question is the question that is not asked; when writing a story, every piece of information can be vital.

In their pursuit of information, they also need to be accurate. You need to tell them how important it is to keep an open mind, to gather facts from a variety of sources, and to check those facts. They need to know that good journalists do not tolerate inaccuracies in spellings, names, dates, locations, and other facts, and that good journalists keep their own feelings out of their stories. This is true whether the stories involve the journalists' best friends or worst enemies, or issues about which the journalists have strong opinions. Remember to also tell them that every story has at least two sides and possibly more, and to make sure the story they write has all sides of the issue expressed in their story.

The students also need to understand that good journalists will write good stories about whatever topic they are assigned to cover, regardless of their interest in the story. Sometimes they realize that even if they are not interested in the story, someone else might be; thus they should write every story like the one they would write about their favorite topic.

Finally, it is important to discuss with the students the reaction to irresponsible journalism. You can illustrate this by using examples of tabloid journalism, but probably you can find examples of irresponsible reporting either in a reporting text or in newspapers available locally.

No matter which techniques you use, you will find that discussing the seriousness of journalism throughout the year will help the students develop a serious attitude toward the subject and toward their publication. It is very important that they demonstrate this, for it will result in a better product and in fewer frustrations for you in your role as the student publications adviser.

CHAPTER 3
Overcoming Irresponsibility

Irresponsible students generally do not conform to even the lowest expectations of their teachers, in terms of common courtesy, attitude about school, and output concerning academic work. These students often lack the politeness to call and cancel appointments they cannot keep, they regularly fail to complete their assigned tasks, and they create unacceptable excuses for not doing what is expected of them; generally, they exert only a minimal amount of effort toward the tasks they do complete. Take precautions to keep such students out of the journalism program or take appropriate actions to rid yourself of this problem if they do slip into your program and cause trouble. Any action taken against a student, however, should be cleared through the school administration beforehand.

Take Precautions

To have irresponsible students as members of a publication staff is a sure bet that you will be heading for unwanted headaches and a very long and stressful semester. Editors cannot assign these students critical tasks, and even relying on them for noncritical work can lead to delays that ultimately will have a major impact on morale and production. Additionally, when some staff members carry an "I don't care" attitude, the damage they can cause to the publication's image (not to mention your image and the image of your class) may be devastating. It is best to identify and remove these students from the staff if they cannot be properly focused in a timely fashion.

If you have followed the suggestions in Chapter 1, concerning the recruitment of responsible and talented students, there is a good chance that you will not have many irresponsible staff members. On the other hand, if the school does not allow you to control the journalism enrollment, the class will probably attract several students who you would rather not have as staff members.

Generally, three types of high school publication programs exist nationwide: some publications are produced in laboratory classes separate from journalism classes; some publications are produced within journalism classes; and some publications are produced as an extracurricular activity. If you cannot control enrollment, make it a point to have several discussions with the guidance counselors or others who have power to place students on the staff or in the journalism classes. In these discussions, impress upon these people how important it is to have responsible students enrolled in the classes wherein publications are produced.

Additionally, early in the school year, it is strongly recommended to have an orientation meeting with the publication(s) editors. This is an opportunity to discuss with them the irresponsibility they can expect from some staff members and the parameters of their authority in dealing with these students. Together, all of you can work out a system for dealing with these minor problems before they become major problems. Some suggestions might include ways to monitor and report counterproductive activity, and steps to be taken by the editors to ensure that the production schedule is not disrupted by the failure of these staff members to do what is expected of them.

While the editors probably know enough to come to the adviser when staff members fail to produce, they may not know how to protect themselves against the situation. Suggest to them that on critical assignments, they can assign two reporters. Thus if one fails partially or completely, the other might have enough material (photographs or copy) to save the story. Also, another suggestion might be that your editors follow up on all assignments, to make sure that none are being left to the last minute. If you have identified irresponsible students, (through experience or other techniques), share this knowledge with the editors, who then can avoid assigning these people critical tasks. Of course, this should be done tactfully and professionally.

Intervene When Necessary

Assuming that the world is not a perfect place and several irresponsible students end up as staff members, do not hesitate to intervene when their behavior interferes with the publication process. Although the editors may possess the technical authority to issue orders, they may lack the ability or the will to take appropriate action. Remember, they are dealing with their peers, while the adviser is the authoritative figure. Also, they may not understand the seriousness of the problems that irresponsible staff members can cause, until it is too late in the production schedule to implement corrective measures.

To avoid such problems, several steps can be taken. First, require all students on the staff to sign contracts that explicitly state what is expected of them. These contracts should be returned to you after they are counter-signed by parents or guardians, as this provides evidence that several people understand the situation. Violation of the contract provides grounds for intervention. An example of this type of contract may be found at the end of this chapter.

Second, at the first class meeting at the beginning of the school year, stress the idea of teamwork. Tell the students that all staff members will be relying on each other, much like workers on an assembly line, and that if one section of the line breaks down, the whole product is jeopardized. Also draw a parallel between student publications work and the efforts of a sports team; tell your students that they must work together for the desired result. You might tell them about the football coach who gave his team sweatshirts with the word "TeAm" printed on the front. The coach said, "You may notice that the m and e are small; that's because there is no me on this team because you are a team and not a bunch of me's."

You might even use the example of a person who has a sore thumb. Remind the students how hard it is to perform even simple manual tasks when the thumb on one hand is sore, and compare the activity of two hands working together with the activity of the staff working together. If there is even one tiny imperfection, affliction, or flaw, the whole process is disturbed.

Finally, be prepared to hold individual conferences with staff members who prove to be incorrigibly irresponsible. Try not to shy away from this task, as the repercussions of their behaviors are unlimited. After a minimal number of chances, if they do not improve, remove them from the staff. Although this may seem to be a harsh punishment, it is much better to remove the problem than it is to submit the rest of the staff to the consequences of such behavior.

While advisers may never understand or get used to the amount of irresponsibility that some students exhibit, be prepared to deal with it swiftly. You will save yourself and your staff much anguish. It isn't a pleasant chore, but it is one which all advisers will encounter in their careers.

SAMPLE CONTRACT FOR PUBLICATION STAFFS

Producing a student publication requires complete dedication from every member of the publication staff. Staff members must be prepared to spend time on the publication during school hours, after school hours, and on some weekends.

Additionally, staff members should understand that because of the significant amount of time required to produce a publication, they need to reduce the amount of time they spend in connection with other school-related activities or outside work.

While editors will spend more time on the publication than will other staff members, students involved in reporting, photography, and production must expect to devote more time to their publication work than they would to a regular class. This is a natural requirement of the journalistic process.

_____

I, _____, understand the obligations of a student publication staff member and agree to meet these obligations to the best of my ability.
Date signed: _____

To Parents:
I give my permission for _____
to become a member of the publication staff. I understand that after-school and weekend work may be necessary.
_____ Date: _____

CHAPTER 4

Enhancing Poor Skills

One of the major arguments for expanding journalism curriculum at the high school level is that journalistic skills also apply to the social and business environments that students encounter later in their lives. Unfortunately for high school journalism advisers, many of the students do not bring these skills with them to the student publication. In fact, except for the editors, many staff members are probably lacking skills in one or more of the following areas: writing and editing, photography, production, planning, administration, leadership, and machine use. Here are some ways you can help eliminate the students' deficiencies.

Writing and Editing Skills

After all has been done to keep poor writers and editors from joining the staff (discuss journalistic requirements with the school administrators and guidance counselors, explain the expectations to students wishing to apply for staff positions, and reject poor writers and editors on the basis of the essays they write as part of their applications for staff positions), the chances are good that you will still face some poor writers and editors. After all, if all the poor writers and editors were weeded out, you might have an extremely small staff.

Furthermore, it is an accepted part of the adviser's job to teach some of these skills to the staff members, and there are many ways to do this. In discussing ways to do this, explain to the students that the terms "writer" and "writing" are used as umbrella terms that encompass both writing and editing skills. Then explain to the staff members that good writing can be the result of good editing.

One technique many advisers employ successfully throughout the year involves the use of writing review sessions. During the first few weeks of the school year, before any significant publication work is done, go ahead and devote small amounts of class time to general rules that student writers commonly violate. Normally, this includes rules of grammar and style, but the sessions also should involve discussions of critical thinking, balanced coverage, and audience characteristics. Later, as the weaknesses of individual writers surface, assign practice exercises that are tailor-made for each staff member's needs. After several issues of the student newspaper have been published, common writing errors will be easily identifiable. To correct most of these problems, create and discuss with the students a "Top 10" errors chart.

While you are conducting the first writing review session, it would be useful to identify the causes of poor writing. High school students generally hear about the symptoms of poor writing (particularly the ones that apply to their own work), but some instructors have found great success in improving the students' writing by discussing the reasons why people write poorly.

Often, poor writing involves careless thinking, lack of attention to the audience, and the inability to listen. Although all three of these problems need to be addressed, the ability to listen is one of the most important skills to be learned and should be discussed in detail.

Unlike creative writing, which is generated primarily from the author's experience and imagination, news writing is generated mostly by interviews with human sources. The student reporters, therefore, must be good listeners who can accurately keep track of and report facts and quotations.

One way to help the staff members become good listeners is to practice active listening exercises with them. To do this, choose a controversial topic and ask one person to verbalize feelings about the topic. Then tell the other students to take notes. Ask one notetaker to paraphrase what the speaker has said. After this has been successfully completed, move to another topic and repeat the process.

In addition to your own efforts in helping the staff members become better writers, enlist fellow teachers from the school to review the students' writing. One way to do this is by asking your colleagues to allow the staff members to write news stories about material covered in class. While the stories will probably not make the student publication, this procedure is good journalistic practice, and it is useful as an academic learning aid for the material being covered in class. This technique is especially useful in classes that traditionally are not writing classes, e.g., math and science.

Another way to enlist aid from other teachers is to ask them to allow the staff members to practice writing skills exercises in class after they have finished the relevant classwork. This is only useful, however, if teachers in your school generally give students time in class to work on assignments. Be careful not to push this technique too aggressively because when students in one class do homework from another class, some teachers become very upset.

One method that is an amusing way to improve writing skills involves the use of publications from rival high schools. At the beginning of the year, arrange with other high school journalism advisers in your area to exchange school newspapers and yearbooks. As the publications arrive, hold critique sessions with staff members and ask them to find examples of good writing and examples of flawed writing. To prime them for this activity, have them critique past issues of their own publication. A wonderful offshoot of this procedure is that when you and the staff members critique the current issue, slyly ask them if they think their counterparts in other schools found the same errors. This creates a kind of peer pressure that can help to build pride in writing good copy for their publication.

If outside peer pressure doesn't prompt the students to take pride in their writing, remind them that there are local, state, regional, and national competitions in which their work will be judged by professional writers and editors. When students know their work will be reviewed and judged by professionals, they often work more diligently at their tasks. Winning a contest is also a great morale booster. Incidentally, the adviser can create smaller-scale competitive rewards by giving periodic recognition to the best news and feature stories in the students' publication. Be careful, however, not to create the impression that you favor certain writers and always reward them with the recognition.

In addition to letting professionals judge the students' work, use good professional writing as a way to teach students how to model their writing after the best. Often, collections of good newswriting can be obtained from outside media institutions, e.g., The Poynter Institute, and from the publishers of prize-winning newspapers, e.g., Knight-Ridder, Inc. and Gannett Co., Inc.

Keep such collections in a publications library in the classroom or in a section of your school's library. Other writing aids also should be placed here, so students may review and use them at their convenience. In addition to collections of prizewinning news stories, other resources may include grammar books, reporting books, and stylebooks.

Regarding stylebooks, the school library should include a stylebook from one of the major U.S. news agencies (Associated Press or United Press International), but an additional stylebook should be specifically created for the students' publication. This should be created at the beginning of the year, preferably with the publications editors' input, and it should clearly explain the writing style and the layout style to be used in the publication. A stylebook of this nature will save everyone a great deal of time, and it will promote consistency and continuity in the final products.

In some instances, a buddy system may be implemented to improve weak writing skills. Pair a good writer with a poor writer and assign them stories that are not too difficult. In graded situations, tell them that each will receive a grade that is an average of the grades earned on their individual stories, as this is an incentive for the good student to help the poor student. Use this technique sparingly, though, for some good writers will resent being used as teachers' aides. Also, the good writer might end up doing the entire story while the poor writer sits and watches.

When all else fails, consider assigning the poor writers tasks that do not involve writing. Ask them what they really would like to do, and from this discussion a hint may be obtained as to what they could do for the publication. These people may be asked to do design and production, to sell advertising, to do bookkeeping, to be involved in distribution, to be in charge of work area tidiness, or to run errands.

Ultimately, try not to spend an inordinate amount of time trying to make a poor writer into a good writer. You will have enough to do without teaching all of the basic English skills to the publication staff.

Photography Skills

Some of the staff members who say they want to be photographers (or that they are photographers) will actually have little or no talent for shooting, developing, or printing pictures. There are a variety of steps to improve the situation if the would-be staff photographers are weak in several relevant areas.

First, it would be a good idea if you could familiarize yourself with the field of photography so you could coach the staff photographers and offer advice to them if they should ask. Knowledge in the photography field can be gained by taking a course in basic photography and/or learning from one of your "expert" friends, or spending time with a local photographer. Attending photography workshops is another option to consider to obtain "expertise" in the field of photography. If none of the options mentioned previously in the paragraph are available, try to read several photography texts so, at the very least, you will know more than the students.

If photography still isn't your strong point, try to convince a local photographer to help out staff members with tips and pointers as to how to take better pictures. If you are fortunate enough to have a staff member who has made a hobby of photography, use that person to help teach others the basics. Do not, however, allow the publications photographers to go unsupervised and have free reign of the darkroom and equipment.

Also, ask some local photographers to come and talk to the staff. While there might not be a professional photographer in the area, someone locally (perhaps even a parent of one of your students) surely will have some expertise in this field. Ask friends and acquaintances about this or prevail upon a local publisher to let a staff photographer visit the class.

Before any pictures are to be taken for the publication, ask the staff photographers for some samples of their work. If they are acceptable, one task has been cleared. If the samples are not acceptable, require ample practice in photography before any critical assignments are given.

Other ways to improve photographic skills are to conduct group critiques of photos in other publications, maintain a photo library for reference purposes, and obtain collections of award-winning photographs to place in the publications library. The National Press Photographers Association and The University of Missouri School of Journalism currently publish an annual collection.

The staff members also may gain insight about photography from the critiques they will receive if their work is entered in regional, state, or national contests. The information, however, may come too late in the year to help current issues, but it may prove useful for improving future publications.

Production Skills

One of the major causes of failing to meet deadlines is the staff's lack of production skills. For many, the experience on a student newspaper or yearbook will be their first encounter with layout and paste-up; these staff members will be learning everything about the different areas while they are actually doing the required tasks.

To improve students' production skills, try to implement the same techniques suggested above for improving the staff members' photography skills, i.e., teach production skills to the staff (if you are capable of doing so), ask professionals to help in this area, and send the students to relevant workshops.

A class field trip to a local print media outlet may help the students learn time-saving design rules and paste-up techniques. Try to arrange visits at two specific times: once during deadline time, so the staff can see a professional in action; and once during a slow period, so the professionals can explain their work thoroughly. After the visits, provide practice time and materials for the students, to enable them to work out problems they will experience. Remember, actual hands-on experience and active participation will be a helpful tool in the entire publication process.

If the students can afford the time to do so, and if you can obtain permission from local media practitioners, arrange for the staff members to "shadow" professional layout and paste-up people during a weekend or school vacation period. During the course of a day or two of this activity, such one-on-one programs can prove to be exciting and educational. Advisers also may obtain information that can be used during the school year.

Additionally, false deadlines can be very beneficial to the students and their publication deadlines. A false deadline will help them by allowing them to redo pages and layouts that have been giving them trouble, thus enabling them to meet "the real deadline" that has been set for them by the editors.

Planning Skills

If you can convince students that planning is a crucial element in the publication schedule, and that they need to create techniques which will ensure the plans will be followed, a lot of difficulties and headaches will be avoided. There are many ways to encourage the development of these attitudes, and several steps can be taken to protect the staff members from their lack of good judgment in this area.

Time management should be at the top of the discussion list when you meet the publication staff at the beginning of the school year. This would be a good first step toward making them aware of both the importance of planning and what can happen when proper time management techniques are not applied.

If you aren't a time management expert, ask a professional manager from the local community to present a guest lecture on this topic. Perhaps someone from a local newspaper or a local college would be a likely candidate for this task, but anyone who agrees to do it should be coached in advance to adapt the presentation to the high school level. Another possibility is to take the students to journalism workshops where professionals discuss planning techniques and requirements. Often, regional or state high school press associations hold conventions at which such workshops are offered.

In areas where professional workshops are not available

able or if the budget doesn't allow these excursions, discuss in class the different ways editors and reporters can achieve their goals. Suggest to the students that they can create mini-deadlines for complex tasks, so completing the entire task will not seem to be as impossible as it originally looks. Keeping a flow chart for task completion is one way to keep tabs on how well schedules are being followed. Posting a publication ladder (an overall chart of page-by-page content) and checking off completed pages may also be used as a way to monitor progress on the entire publication.

Another step that can be considered is to require the staff members to create their own task completion schedules and provide them to the adviser. By requiring progress reports, you can periodically check up on each student. To help the students create such schedules, hold staff meetings and involve everyone in the process.

One eye-opening technique, to help the staff members realize just how long completing an assignment will take, is to ask them to predict the amount of time they will spend on their first assignment. Then require them to keep track of the time they actually spend on that assignment. Often, they will be amazed at how far short their predictions fall.

Rewarding staff members for completing their work early and penalizing them for completing their work late also can be an effective method in encouraging good planning. In graded situations, homework that is turned in early could be awarded bonus points, while homework turned in late will have points deducted. For publication staffs whose work is not graded, rewards may take the form of extra privileges, time off, and parties. Conversely, in these situations, penalties may include extra work on weekends, withholding of bylines, and dismissal from the staff. It should be noted, however, that dismissal of a student should be used as a last resort.

Eventually, after most of these exercises, a majority of the students will develop planning skills, but some will fail to follow through on their plans. For example, during the organized chaos that occurs during deadline week, some students will attempt to "goof-off." Two frequently used methods of goofing-off, which defy easy detection, include taking extra time for out-of-room assignments and "roving purposefully" around the room after an assignment is completed.

To avoid the first problem, create and use check-out sheets for students who are asked to do out-of-room interviews, advertising sales, or errands. These sheets should contain columns for the student's name, the assignment given, the time the student left, and the time the student should return. Either you or an editor should monitor the sheets closely.

To avoid the "roving" problem, staff members should be given several tasks to complete so they never have the luxury of feeling that their work is completed. As with the check-out sheets, each student's progress must be monitored closely to make sure each staff member always has something to do.

Without continual monitoring, only half the staff will be working on the publication at any one time. The other half will be either walking the halls or goofing off.

To lift some of the monitoring burden from yourself, delegate some of these tasks to your editors. Choose appropriate editors for monitoring, and discuss the situation so each will know what to expect. For example, the managing editor can be in charge of monitoring out-of-room editorial assignments, the copy editor can be in charge of in-class writing assignments, the photography editor can be in charge of photography activity, the production editor can be in charge of in-class design and paste-up activity, and the advertising manager can be in charge of out-of-class sales activity.

In spite of all the activities designed to develop the students' planning skills and to ensure that they carry out their plans, there still will be occasions when students will let each other down. As precautionary steps, in addition to everything else that has been suggested in this section, a concerted effort must be made to realize students need more guidance than you actually think. Try to recognize these problems before they become serious, and build in "lost days" in the publication calendar. Given the other steps that can be taken, these preventive measures may be enough to keep the staff on schedule.

Administrative Skills

Although you may have had a good deal of experience with administrators, and although you may be a capable administrator, students generally will not possess administrative skills. To run a smooth operation, at least two of the editors must learn to be capable administrators. Thus if one is absent or leaves the staff, another will be able to continue the process unimpeded.

The best way to start this process in motion is to discuss sample administrative problems with your designated student administrators. Let them know what can go wrong and how to prevent such things from taking place. Out-of-class meetings with the student administrators may be the best way to educate them as to their daily roles and their special roles in problem situations.

As part of their training, help them create instruction sheets that describe common procedures to be followed when completing certain tasks. Such tasks might include maintaining and ordering supplies, preparing materials for delivery to the printer, and keeping track of advertising sales, payments, and commissions.

Although this process may be somewhat difficult to implement, educate them carefully and supervise their work closely for the first few weeks, until you are convinced they can handle their administrative responsibilities. Throughout the year, conduct spot checks and hold regular meetings with them to check their progress. At these times you will be able to address any concerns they may have.

One other type of administrative skill that many of the staff members may have to develop involves personnel skills. Those staff members who will be interacting with school employees, whether to complete a story or to conduct publication business, must learn to treat these people courteously and responsibly. It is a good idea to hold orientation sessions for new staff members who will have frequent assignments or duties that involve school personnel. It also is a good idea to introduce the school personnel to the staff who will be seeking their cooperation on a regular basis.

Leadership Skills

The elusive quality of leadership is something that the publication editors may have to develop. Encourage this by example, and in conversation, and make sure it is discussed thoroughly with those whom you think would make good leaders.

One way to identify potential leaders is to ask other teachers about the students you share with them. This is particularly useful for a new faculty member; most teachers will be happy to make recommendations, and they will be pleased that you considered them for this selection process.

Another way to identify potential leaders concerns the use of problem-solving tests involving small groups. (This can either be beneficial or detrimental to the process.) Often, when a group leader is not designated, a leader will emerge. Problem-solving tests should include tasks related to the publication, such as how to raise more funds, how to generate more student body interest, or how to avoid missing deadlines.

Additionally, by stressing the role of adviser, you may force the editors to assume more leadership responsibilities. During the first editorial board meeting of the year, which should take place before the beginning of the school year, make sure to stress that you are not an editor and that the student editors are to manage the publication. Make it clear to the staff that you will offer advice and that you will on occasion run interference for them when they have trouble with others who are not directly involved in the publication. But make sure to remind them that the role of the adviser is not to be a working staff member.

To clarify your role and the roles of the editors, it is advisable to provide them with a detailed, written job description for each staff position. This will give them the opportunity to know clearly what is expected of them, for the job descriptions should include references to chains of command and supervision.

Certainly, to encourage leadership throughout the school year, reward it periodically by giving recognition to those who provide it. Such reward may take as simple a form as posting staff members' names or as complex a form as showing trust in the editors by discussing with them information not publicized to the entire staff. The information might involve plans for the publication or its staff, criticism of the publication, or semi-private news unrelated to the publication.

Machine Skills

Many machines are used in producing student publications, and very often, students have not had contact with such machines prior to becoming staff members. Machines as simple as typewriters and as complex as computers and laser printers are now part of today's high school journalism program, and more than one person on the staff has to know how to operate them. To ensure that progress will not be held back by the staff's inability to use these necessary machines, a number of steps may be taken.

First, if at all possible and with few exceptions, require the ability to type as a prerequisite for membership on the editorial staff. This will mean that most of the staff writers will have keyboarding skills which can be applied to computers as well as to typewriters.

Second, teach as many students as possible to operate the machines used continually as part of the journalistic process at your school, no matter how simple or complex they are. This holds true for the photography area as well as for the editorial and production areas. Of course, as the adviser, make sure you know how to operate every machine the students will come into contact with, even if it requires after-school training. It is okay to rely on students to train other students, but know what to do in case you are called upon for help. Once again, consider asking an expert to visit the class and give a guest lecture on the operation of certain equipment. The expert might be a local photographer (who could discuss techniques of bulk loading, photojournalism, developing, and printing), a representative of the company from which the machines were obtained, or a member of the school's clerical staff who operates such machines daily.

In smaller schools, where there might not be many mechanical facilities or a large number of students who have machine skills, try a third technique. Make a deal with the business teacher and some business students, to guarantee that the publication work will be completed without too much stress.

When the staff has typing or duplication needs, business students are likely candidates to ask for help. In return, they might receive free publications, a limited number of free photographs of themselves, monetary reimbursement for their time, or recognition in the publication. If a monetary reimbursement is decided upon, make sure there are strict guidelines involved and that there isn't overpayment for services rendered.

Use of non-journalism students to perform tasks the publication staff needs to have done should be reserved for desperate situations. High school is an excellent place for students to learn basic machine skills relevant to journalism, and if at all possible, they should be required to do so.

Finally, in schools that have a small number of one-of-a-kind machines (ditto machines, mimeograph machines, photocopiers) that are closely guarded by zealous administrators, try to work out an arrangement whereby only two of the staff members are thoroughly trained to use the machines. These students would be "checked out" on the machines by those in charge of the facilities, so everyone involved would feel secure in the limited access that would be allowed.

No matter what kind of skills are involved, you will find there is always room for improvement. Sometimes, the speed with which the students will acquire or improve their skills will be surprising. When setbacks are experienced, discount them as learning experiences and plod forward toward the next challenge. Good advisers expect more than what is achieved.

CHAPTER 5
Combatting Unrealistic Expectations

Students with unrealistic expectations occasionally decide to join a publication staff. This occurs because either they have completed the prerequisites for joining the staff or they have decided that working on and being a part of the newspaper or yearbook staff would be fun. The students often overestimate their own abilities and underestimate the demands of the journalistic process that is required of them. They also may not appreciate the relationship of the publication to the adviser and to those not directly involved in its production. As adviser, make sure to take precautions to help such students comprehend the reality of the situation.

Student Abilities

New staff members sometimes overestimate their own abilities because of several different reasons: 1) because other teachers have praised their writing, 2) because they have never tried to meet the requirements of a student publication, or 3) because they have not been challenged by former instructors when it has come to writing and grammar. Some staff members may think journalistic writing is the same as the writing they have completed in English classes, or they may think journalistic writing, in general, is easy.

One way to help new staff members realize the difference between writing essays or reports and writing news or feature stories is to draw a clear distinction between the two types of writing. Early in the school year, hold a special session for the new staff members. During this meeting give them handouts and discuss the topic of journalistic writing. Emphasize the fact that to be considered a responsible journalist, both writing and reporting skills are necessary. Also tell them that being good at one does not necessarily mean being good at the other.

Another way to introduce the differences between reporting and writing is to actually demonstrate journalistic writing to them. To do this, give each new staff member a reporting assignment and have him or her complete the task and turn in the assignment. After you have reviewed all the completed stories, be as devastating as possible in the remarks about style and content that were found in the students' stories. This technique may let the air out of many overinflated egos, but this can be adjusted as the individual situation dictates. Be careful to avoid chasing potentially good writers away from the publication with this technique. Saving this method for later in the semester might work, particularly when overbearing new staff members need to find out that they are not as talented as they think they are.

Regardless of the approach, you will find that new students who are subjected to the "orientation" technique, the "assignment" technique, or both, will turn in stories which are better written and more complete than they would have been without such education.

The Journalistic Process

Perhaps it is to be expected that people who have seen only the finished product do not realize how much effort goes into the process that produces it. This is true in the professional world of journalism and is the case in the high school journalism setting. Among many high students, there seems to be a pervasive attitude that journalism is easy.

In addition to the suggestions made in the planning section contained in Chapter 4, there are other steps which can help new staff members realize how difficult it is to produce a publication. One step is to acknowledge during the first day of class that all of the hard work put in by the staff members is necessary. Also provide examples of the problems that can occur, and ask either the current editor or a former editor to provide examples from their past experiences as to what it takes to produce a student publication.

One idea to consider might be to invite a media professional or a local college publication adviser to the class to point out the interrelationship among tasks performed during the journalistic process. From the guest speaker's presentation, staff members should understand how critical each person's work is to the whole, and how a problem in one area often creates problems in another area.

Cite the example of when a photographer accidentally ruins the only existing film of an important event. Layouts have to be redone, copy may have to be readjusted, and paste-up may have to start over. Another example might be when a story is not completed before deadline, space in the publication reserved for that story must be taken up by something else. Tell the students that a blank hole in the publication will not be tolerated and somehow must be filled. Someone on the staff (make sure this isn't you) has to take time to make the adjustments, and that slows down the process. A less complex example concerns the amount of time it takes to correct simple typographical errors in copy.

The main point that the guest speaker should make is that the journalistic process takes longer than most people would imagine; even a simple problem sometimes takes an inordinate amount of time to correct. The new staff members need to understand that the process is an ongoing one of playing "catch up" with a deadline, before they can appreciate the amount of time and effort it takes to succeed in the journalistic game.

Expectations About Others

If the students have not been educated to think otherwise, they will believe that the adviser is merely a high-powered member of the publication staff. They also will

16

believe that everyone in the school is interested in the publication and that others not directly involved in it will be fully cooperative. To ensure that these beliefs are dispelled immediately, provide the staff members with some personnel training, which should commence with a handout at the beginning of the school year.

The handout should be a description of the role of the adviser, and it should clearly indicate what the adviser will do and not do for the publication. This topic is discussed more thoroughly in Chapter 16, but it is important enough to mention several times. The students need to understand that you are not an editor, a writer, or a photographer, and that they will be expected to carry the load. If this is not made clear to them at the outset of the semester, expect to act as the "super staff" member for the entire year. If for some reason this does occur, take steps to correct it in subsequent semesters.

Another aspect of personnel education that has to do with the role of the adviser concerns the students' expectations about grading. While discussing the role as adviser, make perfectly clear the fact that grades (for those advisers whose graded journalism classes produce publications) will be given according to quality and volume of output. Explain to them that good grades will not be handed out for just showing up for class. There are several ways to handle evaluation and grading, and they are discussed more thoroughly in Chapter 17.

Also discuss with the students the fact that administrators generally view the publication as a potential problem which needs to be watched closely. In fact, some administrators merely tolerate student publications as necessary evils mandated by a higher authority. Consider yourself lucky if the administration looks favorably upon the school's publications, and allows the students adequate funding, facilities, and freedom of the press.

Additionally, teachers and other students may ignore the publication or in other ways appear to be apathetic toward it. While staff members may think journalism is the greatest experience in high school, they must also realize that their enthusiasm often will not be matched by other teachers or fellow students. This may cause a morale problem, but if the staff members realize in advance that this may happen, it will help them carry on in spite of it.

Community members may cause another problem, especially if they are the ones who are asked to support your publication financially. Occasionally they will fail to purchase advertising the students expect them to buy, and sometimes individuals won't pay the bills the publications advertising manager sends them. Again, make the students aware of the possibilities, so the reality won't cause too much damage to the publication.

Finally, inform the staff members that professional photographers, typesetters, publishers, and publishers' representatives don't always do what they say they will do. Although problems with these people are infrequent, they do occur. Generally, because they want to continue doing business with the publication, problems are easily solved; sometimes, however, it may take time and many telephone calls before you and the students obtain satisfaction.

The solutions for most of the problems caused by the unrealistic expectations of the students take the form of preventive measures, and in the role of adviser, you will find that many problems can be defused by talking about them before they occur. This means constantly being aware of a potential problem and realizing when the situation is ready to erupt. Give a good deal of thought to the possibilities likely to materialize, given your individual situation.

CHAPTER 6
Making the Most of Dysfunctional Staff Members

There are many ways in which the behavior of staff members can disrupt the production of a student publication. While advisers can deal with most problems quickly and successfully, certain students will be chronically dysfunctional because they have short attention spans, an inability to grasp concepts important to the journalistic process, or indifferent attitudes toward scholastic journalism. What sets these students aside from others who weaken the operation is that often they cannot be properly educated to overcome their deficiencies. Generally, these students will be identifiable, so work with them to see which ones can fit into the operation in some way, and dismiss the ones who can't be helped in the time you can devote to them.

Short Attention Spans

Students who join a high school publication are teenagers, and you will find that many of the staff members cannot or do not keep their minds on any one project for reasonable amounts of time. This is unfortunate because the journalistic process often requires prolonged attention to single tasks. To guarantee that work on the publication will be done and done correctly, identify the problem students and work to improve their attention spans.

The first step that should be taken is to assign small tasks to each new staff member and monitor the amount of time each student takes to complete the assignment. Taking into consideration the quality of the work that is completed, assign increasingly larger tasks to the students whose work is done quickly and correctly. After a short series of assignments, identifying the students who need help on their attention spans should be relatively easy.

When you have decided that some staff members cannot complete projects that take a good deal of time and concentration, it will be to your advantage to evaluate their abilities and interests. Often, these students will be satisfied to complete an ongoing series of small tasks, and they may have the ability to work in a variety of areas. Their abilities also may be related to their interests. Thus if you can identify the journalistic tasks they specifically like, their attention spans may increase and the tasks may be completed more thoroughly than you would have imagined. While it is important to allow all of your staffers to choose their tasks whenever possible, it is particularly important to allow staffers with short attention spans to do so.

Sometimes there are not enough small tasks available to keep everyone busy. If this is one of your problems, work with your editors to break large tasks into smaller sections. You will find that some students (editors in particular) feel they need to be in control of entire projects, and that they have to do all of the work associated with such projects. When this happens on a publication staff, the effect is a shift of the work load from the many to the few, preventing some students from doing work they could do. If you are watchful concerning this type of situation, you may avoid burnout on the part of your editors. Usually, you will have plenty of small tasks available for those students who need them.

If you find that your editors are constantly running out of small tasks, you might suggest to them that they ask a pair of staffers to work together on an assignment. While the pairing itself may be a problem, when two compatible students work together, both often pay more attention to the task, even if it isn't something they would normally volunteer to do. The result is that staffers are kept busy, work gets done, and attention spans are increased. Naturally, supervision is an important ingredient in the success of such projects, so you need to set aside extra time when you have more than a few students working in pairs.

Whether your students have short attention spans or not, always be sure to reward task completion. The reward can be as simple as a verbal pat on the back, but it is important to acknowledge these accomplishments. Other rewards include giving time off from publication work, assigning desirable tasks to those whose work is done well and on time, and providing occasional refreshments for your staff.

In cases where you have little or no success with students who have short attention spans, you may have to assign exercises that improve concentration. If you cannot create simple journalistic exercises that can be completed in short amounts of time, contact your school counselors or the school psychologist for ideas or existing exercises. When this does not help, it is time for you to remove your problem students from the staff, for they will cause more disruption than other staffers can tolerate. Don't be afraid to take this step, but be prepared to produce written records of the problems you have encountered with these students. Such records should include your summaries of the students' performances on assigned tasks, copies of unsatisfactory work the students have done, and copies of letters you have sent to the students' parents (in which you make note of the problems you have not been able to solve).

One measure you can take that might prevent students with short attention spans from becoming publication staff members is to discuss with your guidance counselors the demands of the publication process. If they know it requires the ability to concentrate on tasks for long periods of time, you may convince them not to place certain students in your classes for credit. In school systems where student publications are noncredit activities, you may convince counselors to discourage certain students from volunteering for the staff.

Another measure that prevents some of the problems

associated with students who have short attention spans is good planning by you and your editors. As a precautionary step, at the beginning of the school year, meet with your editors, discuss the possibility of problem staffers with them, and ask them to create a very long list of small tasks that could be assigned to staff members who cannot satisfactorily complete long projects. Being prepared for such situations will save everyone a lot of agony.

Inability to Grasp Concepts

Although some students may not have acceptable attention spans, others who are able to concentrate for long periods of time may not have the ability to learn the skills necessary to perform competently as staff members. This will be evident from the work they turn in, and these students must be dealt with in ways similar to those described in the earlier portion of this chapter. If you have discussed with your guidance counselors the requirements of being a staff member, then you may not have to deal with this type of student.

If for some reason you do have such students, after you have identified them, you will want to hold individual conferences with them to determine what, if anything, they will be able to do for the publication. Before holding these conferences, you may want to review their records to determine if the students have learning handicaps that have been documented.

If you choose to work with these students for awhile, you will want to clearly define for them your expectations concerning their behavior. This will pave the way for you to dismiss them from the staff if they do not measure up to such expectations. You may require them to complete writing exercises or other journalistic exercises, you may want to use them to run errands, and you may have them work in pairs to complete certain tasks.

Naturally, you should give them encouragement when they complete work satisfactorily, but you also should maintain records of their unsatisfactory output. Additionally, you need to make their parents and their counselors aware of the situation as early in the term as possible, in the event that you foresee dismissing a student from the staff. While this step is an unpleasant one, you must not fail to take it when circumstances dictate.

Indifferent Attitudes

Perhaps even more frustrating than students who have the disabilities mentioned above are the students who just don't seem to care about the publication. This problem is more severe than a mere motivational problem, and students who exhibit it must be weeded out quickly before they destroy the morale of your entire staff.

Frequently, these students will be superb achievers in other classes, but they will believe that journalism is an activity to be taken lightly. If your opening speech, in which you discuss the importance of journalism and the seriousness of student publication work, does not inspire these students to re-evaluate their thinking and their behavior, you will need to hold conferences with them to discuss your expectations of them. In these meetings, plainly describe the consequences of indifference, which should include the possibility of dismissal from the staff.

When these students do not satisfactorily complete their assigned tasks, keep records of their work, send memos to their counselors, and write letters to their parents. Keep copies of everything relevant to their performances, and use these copies as evidence when you ask these students to leave the staff. Don't wait very long to take action against incorrigible students, for they can do more damage in a short amount of time than you can correct in an entire school year.

Generally, dysfunctional staff members disrupt publication programs in two ways: physically and emotionally. If their inabilities and their indifference go unchecked, you and all of your staff members will suffer. Because it is your job to minimize the amount of damage such students can do, you must constantly watch out for them and swiftly deal with them when they are identified.

CHAPTER 7
Personal Conflict, Jealousy and Self-Interest

Whenever young people work together in a competitive operation (primarily the high school atmosphere), there is a possibility that interpersonal problems between the students will arise. This possibility will have a greater chance of increasing when an arbitrary power structure is created to govern the operation. Student publications, with their built-in deadline pressures, competitive atmosphere, and editorial power structure, are ideal spawning grounds for interpersonal problems. Advisers must do all they can to prevent and alleviate such problems that will arise during the academic year.

Personal Conflict and Jealousy

While jealousy may cause personal conflict, it is not the only source of conflict among students of a high school publication. Sometimes, conflict occurs when staff members do not meet the expectations of editors, when editors have editorial disagreements concerning content or design, and when communication breaks down among all involved in the publication operation. A variety of other causes, as numerous as individuals on a given publication staff, also exists.

On the other hand, jealousy generally has fewer causes, but it can be equally devastating to an operation if it continues unchecked. Usually, when jealousy is present among the staff members of a student publication, it can be linked to favoritism (either real or perceived) or unequal distribution of power.

To prevent personal conflict and jealousy from causing trouble among the staff members, the adviser must make a strong statement about such issues at the beginning of the school year. Tell the staff members that petty arguments will not be tolerated, and make sure to stress the team approach to completing the necessary work. On the first day of school, introduce the editors to the rest of the staff and acknowledge their power to make decisions about the publication. By doing so, all staff members will realize that you endorse the power of the editors to make assignments and to choose publication content and design. This will also give the students a taste of how a professional publication is managed and what the chain of command involves.

Additionally, conduct training sessions with the editors to sensitize them to the possibility of conflict among staff members. During these initial meetings, point out the importance of not playing favorites, keeping the lines of communication open among staff members, and obtaining suggestions from everyone on the staff. While they may already realize that such conflict might occur, discussing these important ideas will show the editors that you also are aware of it and this may help them to deal with it openly.

As the adviser, keep alert to the rumblings of a building conflict, and deal with them immediately. Don't wait for them to become explosions. A good idea would be to meet with the students, both individually and together. Give them a chance to air their grievances privately, so the entire staff isn't drawn into the conflict. Some staff members will undoubtedly be aware of the problem, but with quick action, the damage caused by this can be limited.

If the conflict has become so pervasive that almost everyone on staff is aware of it, a mandatory staff meeting should be called to air the problems and settle the differences that any staff member may have with fellow students or the publication. This idea should only be attempted when a solution between the parties involved has been ironed out or a settlement is close to being agreed upon. Otherwise, complete chaos might develop and have a negative effect on what the meeting was all about. A general staff meeting would also provide a good opportunity to remind students about your position on conflict among staff members.

When deadline pressures are causing an undue amount of tension among the staff members, quickly try to reduce this pressure by all means possible. Holding a "crazy awards" party often is one useful way to break the tension. To do this, designate categories of comic awards that are unique to the staff. The idea is to prey upon the students' idiosyncrasies to make them laugh at themselves. Provide some snacks and soft drinks to create a party atmosphere.

Another way to reduce the tension is to make the staff exercise together for five minutes. These exercises can combine stretching, running in place, jumping, and deep-breathing exercises. This is a good way to relieve stress, and group exercise usually will create good feelings among your staff members.

While personal conflict may be handled quite easily if it is not allowed to grow into a large-scale war, jealousy may not be solved with such ease. Frequently, jealousy is directly tied to an individual's personality, whereas personal conflict often is linked to a situation. That is why it is particularly important for everyone to know in advance that the editors have your backing. It is also important to explain to staff members that editors have been chosen because of their specific talents and because you believe they will make the best judgments where publication decisions are concerned.

Often, identifying jealousy between staff members is not as easy as it seems. Thus at the earliest possible time of the school year, discuss the jealousy issue with the students. This discussion is especially critical if two or more students apply for the same positions on the staff, or if you know from past associations with some students that they are likely to perceive favoritism in the operation, whether or not it exists.

Make every effort to sensitize the publications editors

to favoritism and the delicate personnel responsibilities of their positions. Likewise, be certain that you are not guilty of favoritism in the role as adviser, because you can also become a source of jealousy among the staff members.

One other technique that is useful in keeping jealousy problems to a minimum is to encourage noncompetitive activities among staff members. Suggest to the editors that they allow staff members to work in small groups, and that the editors change the makeup of the groups occasionally to prevent opportunities for destructive competition.

As soon as problems of jealousy are detected, talk privately with those students involved. Try to determine the source of the problem and whether or not the problem is real or imaginary. In some instances, individual counseling may be required with some students, and in severe cases, outside professional counseling may be desired. In any event, do not let the jealousy problem continue, for it will lead to staff disruptions and a breakdown in operation.

If preventive measures are taken to avoid personal conflict and jealousy among the staff members, and if these problems are handled in a quick professional manner, then the operation will not become deadlocked by favoritism and power struggles. Success in avoiding such problems will allow more time to deal with other serious problems likely to occur during the course of the school year.

Self-Interest

Another type of conflict that student publications advisers must watch for concerns the self-interest of staff members as individuals and as a group. While individual self-interest may lead to problems of personal conflict and jealousy, group self-interest may antagonize large segments of the entire school.

Individual self-interest makes editors into tyrants. Editors who are driven by self-interest will publish their own work and their friends' work instead of the work of other staff members, regardless of quality. Additionally, such editors will consistently take choice assignments for themselves or give choice assignments to their friends, while the most troublesome or tedious assignments are reserved for other staff members. Simply put, individual

self-interest is one of the chief causes of favoritism and power abuse on a publication staff.

Similarly, group self-interest refers to the favoritism and abuse that an entire staff heaps upon its audience. When this happens, only certain activities are covered in the publication, and often an inordinate amount of space is dedicated to certain students in the school. The activities covered are generally those in which publication staff members are involved; the students mentioned in the coverage are generally friends of the publication staff. Naturally, such self-interest is readily evident to the student and adult audiences who read the publication. This type of coverage will reflect poorly upon the publication, the staff members and the adviser.

Obviously, neither of these types of self-interest must be allowed to govern the publication. If your opening day speech has not effectively curbed the self-interest of the staff members, make sure to occasionally remind the editors of their responsibilities in this area. If you are able to keep the editors from giving in to their own self-interests, then the staff members and the publication's audience will not become victims of editorial tyranny. Sometimes, complaints will filter in from staff members that their assignments are always the most boring ones or the ones that must be done after school or on weekends, thus causing them constant inconvenience. These type of complaints should raise a red flag that the editors are falling prey to their worst judgment. In a subtle way, mention these complaints to the editors and pay closer attention to the assignments that are handed out by the editors.

In some cases, staff members who are not editors may also need to be reminded of the self-interest issue, for they may be guilty of allowing their interests to interfere with their work on the publication. This will show up in their choices of stories and in their choices of people quoted in those stories. This may not be evident to the editors, but with a studied reading of several stories by the same person, some patterns may develop. It is very easy for some staff members to put their friends into print, and some may see nothing wrong with this practice until its flaws are pointed out to them.

To help turn self-interest aside, suggest story ideas to those editors with particularly narrow vision. Also, recommend interviews with people the editors may not think to contact. Finally, when editors assign stories to staff members, think about suggesting a variety of story angles, so the students don't pursue the most obvious angle.

Another method that can be useful is to critique the publication in terms of its breadth of coverage. Stress to the staff members the need to cover as many aspects of the school as possible. Not only is that a proper journalistic goal, but it is frequently a measure of publication quality, as judged by professionals when the student publication is entered in editorial contests. On the one hand, the publication should serve all members of the school, either directly or indirectly, by covering as wide a variety of activities and as many people as possible. After all, it does belong to the students. On the other hand, just for the sake of reputation and staff morale, it would be good for the publication to win some kind of award, and good breadth of coverage will help.

If the types of self-interest that interfere with the optimal operation of the students' publication can be discouraged, many problems that result from such interference will be eliminated. If a team approach to responsible journalism is encouraged, you will breed the professional pride that makes a student publication fun to advise.

CHAPTER 8
Teaching Students to Accept Criticism

Although staff members, in many ways, may be ideal workers, sometimes they will resist criticism of the work they have done either individually or as a group. This problem is common in situations involving a new adviser, especially if the adviser is also new to the school system. If the game plan is to be an active adviser who offers constructive criticism, take some precautions before generating a lot of hard feelings and making enemies of your staff members.

To defuse a potentially explosive situation, spend time at the beginning of the year discussing with the staff members the role of criticism in the journalistic process. Explain to them that it is a necessary and accepted part of journalism, and that there are several professional publications dedicated to improving professional journalism through constructive criticism. In fact, ask the school library to subscribe to *The Quill, Columbia Journalism Review*, or another such publication, so the students may see first hand the course that journalistic criticism takes.

To strengthen the argument about the role of criticism in journalism, ask a media professional to visit the staff to discuss this topic and lend credibility to the criticism argument. Encourage the guest speaker to present a survey of the types of criticism that take place in professional journalism, as there are many entertaining examples that may be used to make relevant points. Also, consider suggesting that the guest critique one or more of the students' publications, to reinforce what has been said in the past.

Another technique is to discuss the role of criticism in the "real world," as it applies to journalism as well as to other segments of society. This could be part of a class discussion of criticism in general, which would allow the staff members to air their opinions and feelings about criticism and being criticized. One of the main goals in such a session would be to make it clear that any criticism that is offered is criticism of the student's work, rather than of the person who has done the work. Often, that distinction is blurred, thus impairing subsequent communication between the person who is doing the critiquing and the person whose work is being critiqued.

Journalism students often have difficulty separating themselves from their work, as the stories they write, the photos they take, and the publications they edit are, in a very real sense, extensions of their egos. Thus they are likely to take criticism personally.

As the adviser, of course, always make sure to set a tone of excellence in journalism. When the students understand that a lot is expected from them and that they are valued staff members, most of them will strive to meet their goals. They also will learn to expect and

"As the adviser, of course, always make sure to set a tone of excellence in journalism. When the students understand that a lot is expected from them and that they are valued staff members, most of them will strive to meet their goals...."

welcome the constructive criticism that is offered, both as they prepare their work and after their work is published.

Another way to make criticism more acceptable is to allow students the opportunities to find their own errors. After their publication comes out, spend some time critiquing it as a group. For more impact concerning specific items, the use of an opaque or overhead projector is a good idea. Encourage them to praise the good aspects of it and to offer suggestions for improving other parts. Frequently, the most obvious mistakes will be pointed out by the staff members during this session; this will allow for more time to be spent on the subtle flaws, which, if corrected, can make the difference between a good publication and a great publication.

During the group critique sessions, be particularly careful to praise improvements and special efforts. The use of positive reinforcement provides recognition for those who have corrected past errors and allows you to show your staff that you do not define your role as merely that of a faultfinder.

When it is necessary to deliver some especially harsh criticism, or if it is necessary to criticize a staff member repeatedly for the same offense, it is better to hold a private conversation with those directly involved than to offer such criticism in a group setting. The comments will be better received and they will do more good if they are handled in this way.

Overall, be sensitive to the feelings of the young staff members, as their egos may not be able to tolerate much public scorn, however light and well intended it may be. Such precautions will keep first year staff members from fleeing the situation. At certain times, you may have to be equally sensitive to the feelings of the seasoned staff members, but if they have been with the staff in previous years, you probably will know the limits of their tolerance for criticism.

If there is consistency to the approach of the criticism and careful selection in the ways that it is delivered, the students will come to accept these observations and respect your judgment. In fact, most of them will look forward to the critiques as another way to improve their group effort.

CHAPTER 9
Preparing for Personnel Changes

When the makeup of the publication staff changes significantly, you may wonder how the remaining students will carry on effectively. This will be true whether the loss of one or more talented staff members is expected or unexpected. There are several precautionary steps that can be taken, however, that will help staff members and advisers prevent a lot of headaches and questions. There also are steps that can be taken to prevent some changes from occurring.

Expected Changes

In some instances, the warning that a student is departing the staff will come with adequate notice. The most obvious cause of departure is graduation, but other reasons for staff members not coming back include family relocation or increases in other obligations that may not take them away from the community. Some students will give plenty of advance notice that they plan to attend a different school in the coming year or that their time will be taken up with other activities.

Even when it is a key person in the operation who is leaving, there is no need for panic if proper steps have been taken to protect against such an occurrence. For example, to guard against the possibility that graduation will gut the editorial board, make a concerted effort not to place seniors in every important position. In schools where it is traditional to have an all-junior or all-senior staff for any given publication, work to change that policy so there is an adequate training program which does not require a fresh start at the beginning of each year.

Another step to take is to cross-train staff members in every important position, so when a few of the editors graduate or leave for other reasons, other students will be able to step into their vacated roles. Essentially, this will develop a nucleus of students who can carry on when their colleagues leave. The cross-training may be accomplished by using a rotation system, by choosing co-editors, or by a simple one-on-one training program in which the editors work with assistants until the assistants become proficient. To improve the chances of this idea succeeding, combine two or more cross-training techniques, depending on the makeup and size of the staff. The choice may depend upon the personalities of certain key students, which may dictate avoidance of co-editorship or one-on-one training.

If procedural manuals have not been developed, require the editors to make these manuals, describing the ways they do their jobs. This material can be an essential portion of any training program. The content of each manual should include such information as names and addresses of important contacts (inside and outside the school system); locations of the materials used by the editor; step-by-step directions for completing the various tasks associated with the position; and a list of helpful hints and precautions concerning job performance. You may need to adjust or embellish an editor's attempt to create such a manual, but it is well worth everyone's time to do this, as it will save future staff members monumental amounts of time in subsequent years. If the editors are not competent enough to complete a procedural manual, then this task will be left to the publications adviser. This task should be completed in time for the next academic year and the incoming class of new students.

Unexpected Changes

While the usual departure of students from the staff is expected, the most devastating changes generally are those that happen without sufficient warning: sometimes students quit without notice or advisers remove them because of inappropriate behavior; sometimes their parents abruptly pull them out of school; sometimes they are incapacitated by illness; and sometimes they die unexpectedly.

Although preventive and corrective measures concerning problems discussed in the preceding chapters will greatly reduce chances that staff members will quit or be removed for disciplinary reasons, unexpected changes in the staff's personnel will occur over the years. Whatever causes such changes, those remaining on staff will have to continue the struggle in spite of the loss. Depending upon the reason a student unexpectedly leaves the staff, there are steps, in addition to the effective ones mentioned above, that can help to ease the transition of duties from one student to another and to make the loss more agreeable.

One method that alleviates problems, regardless of the reason for leaving, is to require all staff members to keep weekly written schedules of their activities, both completed and planned, and to file the schedules with the adviser on Mondays or Fridays. Explain the necessity of this procedure in terms of a normal journalistic operation (or any professional operation); those staff members who might have seen the requirement as busy work will be more likely to view it as an aid that ensures orderliness. Thus if anyone leaves the staff abruptly, that person's schedule already will have been mapped out in advance. This reduces the chances that work will be unnecessarily duplicated and allows other staff members to keep appointments that have been made.

Additionally, if a key staff member quits or is removed, it often is a good idea to hold a formal staff meeting and discuss the reasons for the decision. This meeting must be conducted so no one's privacy rights are violated, as this can be a problem in some instances. Generally, the reason someone quits or is removed has something to do with public aspects of the work associated with the publication, and chances are good that some details are known already by the staff. A formal meeting allows the clarification of any misconceptions about the situation and reinforces attitudes about working on a publication staff. Well before any action is taken to remove a student from the class, be certain to learn the school's requirements and procedures for doing so.

Personnel changes caused by illness or death may be tactfully used to promote the staff's dedication to their work. Naturally, in tragic cases, make sure to allow for a period of adjustment before rallying the staff with a "win one for the Gipper" approach, but use every means of tact and sensitivity to make the best of a personal misfortune without being offensive. This can be a very difficult situation for an adviser to be involved with directly. Make sure to use good judgment when approaching it and ask for help if there is a need for it.

If students indicate a desire to leave the staff because they have either lost interest in the publication or because they feel less a part of the group than others who are involved, take the time to speak with these students individually. Reminding them of the contracts that have been created and that they have signed will sometimes keep students from leaving the staff in the middle of a term, but there is no guarantee this ploy will work. Working the unhappy staff members into the mainstream of the journalistic process is often the best way to prevent an immediate withdrawal, although it is sometimes not possible to change the mind of a student determined to leave.

As the adviser, make sure to do all you can to prevent staff members from arriving at this state of mind. Constant vigilance is not enough, although it certainly helps to identify problems at an early stage. In addition to merely watching for problems to develop, constantly strive to convince the shy staff members, who are likely to lose interest because they end up on the fringes of the operation, that they are important to the publication and that they can contribute significantly. Taking preventive measures against learned helplessness ("journalism is so complicated that I can't possibly do all that is required in order to succeed") will save some staff members from

feeling lost, and this is important. Provide such people with positive reinforcement and dispel their fears as soon as these fears are brought to your attention.

During your career as an adviser, many staff members will depart for numerous reasons. While no crystal ball will predict all of the personnel changes the staff will experience, there are ways to prevent some of them from occurring. Also, with good planning, the staff can be prepared to carry on the work despite the departures that can't be prevented. No personnel change will be overly devastating if you constantly work to combat its repercussions and keep a sense of humor.

SECTION II

SOLVING PROBLEMS ASSOCIATED WITH ADVISERS

CHAPTER 10

Sustaining Motivation and Enthusiasm

Although the adviser is the school's primary cheerleader for journalism classes and student publications, the cheerleader's motivation and enthusiasm may occasionally wane. This is true because it is a gigantic undertaking to maintain a high energy level when constantly facing the large number of problems that plague journalism advisers. Nonetheless, because one of the top priorities is to avoid adviser burnout, here are some suggestions to prevent it from occurring.

Make Your Job Pleasant

The attitude that is maintained toward the job can be buoyed by the structure of the position and the "perks" that are included in that structure. The easier the job is for the adviser, the easier it will be to make the school term flow well for everyone.

Whether or not the student publication that is under your guidance is an integral portion of a journalism class you teach, make an ongoing effort to convince administrators to reduce the size of your classes. This is especially true if there are other subjects that must be taught in addition to journalism, as the time spent outside of journalism merely is time taken away from performing the publication advising duties. The argument that can be made is that it takes an inordinate amount of time to advise a student publication properly, compared to sponsoring chess club or some similar social activity within the school. The more students that must be dealt with outside the realm of journalism, the more impossible it becomes to do an adequate job as adviser.

This same argument can be applied to the extra duties most teachers are assigned during their "free" time. Lobby school administrators concerning lunchroom detail, study hall monitoring, and extracurricular duties (e.g., acting as monitor during sporting events or chaperoning dances), to make them reduce your responsibilities in these areas. Reducing some of these obligations will make life less pressured and less stressful.

Whatever success that is accomplished in reducing the time spent outside the journalistic endeavor, also try to make certain that the school administrators will allow you to attend journalism workshops and seminars, even when they are held on school days. It is not unreasonable to expect support for these activities, both in terms of time off and expenses. Such breaks from teaching will help your attitude, improve your abilities and recharge your batteries before tackling the school publication adviser role once again.

Additionally, attending workshops and seminars allows the chance to make easy contacts with other professionals in the journalism field. It always is supportive to know you are not alone in the fight to maintain sanity, and the exchanging of information with other advisers will provide mental and spiritual relief. If the seminars and activities include media professionals as speakers or members of the audience, the experiences can be doubly rewarding because there is a chance these same professionals will consent to being guest speakers for the publication staff.

Guest speakers are particularly important in the fight against sagging motivation because they allow a break from teaching and often serve to recharge the students' enthusiasm (which has an effect on the adviser's enthusiasm as well). The professionals may also offer ideas that can help transform dull journalistic tasks into moderately exciting tasks.

Another way to make the job more pleasant is to delegate as much responsibility as possible. There is a tendency on the part of school publication advisers to maintain close control over every aspect of the operation, sometimes to the point of doing almost all of the nonjournalistic tasks themselves. This is not necessary and it is not a healthy practice, for this will not allow enough time in your life to maintain proper happiness and sanity.

Students and school personnel can handle much of the day-to-day drudgery that may accompany the operation, and this will allow the adviser more time for important and exciting chores. There is no need, for example, to assume more clerical tasks than already assigned. Periodically, of course, check up on the people to whom these duties have been delegated and make sure they are finishing the tasks that have been delegated to them.

Something that always helps to provide a lift to advisers and their staff members is outside recognition of their work. The role of the adviser can be made much more pleasant if the students' publications win awards, so make a concerted effort to enter the students, their work, or both, in at least two contests per year. Some contests are sponsored by national journalism organizations, while others are arranged by scholastic journalism associations in various regions or individual states. If you are unaware of any contests in your geographic area, check with university professors, other high school advisers, and media professionals in the area. Someone is sure to know about the local or regional contests that exist. The contests may be performance contests, which require that students travel to a given place to participate, or they may be the type that requires the students' work to be submitted and then rated by a panel of judges. In either case, the rewards these contests offer are often well worth the effort entering takes.

If there are no contests available in the area, make it a point to send the staff members' work to the competitions offered by professional journalism organizations or the various national scholastic journalism ratings associations in the United States, whose names and addresses are provided in the back of this handbook. The recognition they offer can increase the respect that is received

from administrators and this will help in lobbying efforts to make your job more pleasant.

Reward Yourself

In addition to making the adviser role more pleasant by manipulating the working environment, motivation and enthusiasm can be sustained by scheduling rewards for yourself during the school year. One way to do this is to give yourself an occasional treat that is related to accomplishments at school. When a particular week has been very hectic, make sure the following weekend is spent trying to relax and doing an activity you enjoy. All too often, journalism advisers become so wrapped up in their work that they neglect their own needs, and this eventually leads to stress and burnout. This stress and burnout can be equally hard on an adviser's family and/or close friends.

Sometimes it is unnecessary to wait for a "natural break," such as a weekend, to occur. All weeknights should not be spent doing school-related work, for this, too, will lead to burnout. Make sure that if school work is constantly taken home for review and grading, at least one weeknight is designated for relaxation or family. This will help you to keep a fresh outlook on school in general and toward your advising activities in particular.

Another good time for rewards, as was suggested earlier in the discussion of student motivation and enthusiasm, is when the staff members meet their deadlines. When this happens, it is good to celebrate both with the students and by yourself; use every possible occasion as an excuse to obtain relief from the everyday routine. The rewards don't have to be big, but they should be frequent.

In fact, there is no need to link all personal celebrations to the deadlines students meet. It is a good idea to set short-term goals for yourself and to celebrate when these goals are attained. You are probably the best judge of how much can be accomplished in a given amount of time, so create a list of goals (some of which should be related to your advising activities) that can be realistically attained, and reward yourself every time these goals are met. This can be a dynamic way to maintain adviser enthusiasm, for it allows advisers to recognize the little victories that escape many of them who focus on the whole rather than on the parts.

If a point is reached at which you cannot feel justified in rewarding yourself for an activity, then think about the rewards that are intrinsic to the academic environment. If the advisory role has been set up properly, you might convince yourself that this job is something you enjoy and that there is a paycheck to go along with the enjoyment and self-satisfaction. Many employees cannot make this statement. Also, remember there are more paid holidays for school teachers than for many other workers. Anticipating time off can be a reward in itself and shouldn't be overlooked.

Regardless of the techniques used to sustain motivation and enthusiasm, success is crucial. The bottom line is that the adviser is a role model for the staff members, and once it becomes evident to them that you have lost interest in the role, they will lose interest in theirs. A high school journalism program cannot survive if that happens. Thus the last comment about an adviser's lack of motivation and enthusiasm is that if you suffer hopelessly from this malady, remove yourself from the situation before you poison the entire program and irrevocably damage student attitudes.

CHAPTER 11

Building Experience and Knowledge

In some school systems, teachers become publications advisers because they have completed journalism majors or minors in college. Most of the time, these graduates intend to teach journalism and advise the school newspaper, the yearbook, or both. In other school systems, the task of advising student publications falls either to the newest teacher or to anyone willing to undertake the responsibility, in spite of the amount of education (usually little or none) that person has in journalism.

If your experience and knowledge concerning journalism is minimal, give serious thought to taking immediate steps to improve the situation before too many weeks of the school year have passed. In fact, try to participate in several helpful activities as soon as you learn that you will be a publication adviser, or at least long before the start of the school year.

Consulting and Reading

One step that should be taken, especially if you are assuming the advisory responsibilities from someone in the school or taking over the program as a new adviser, is to consult with the person who is leaving the program. This person should be able to explain important information about the publication program and point out any potential pitfalls specific to the staff and to the operation.

Whether assuming responsibility for an ongoing program or initiating a new program, one way to increase journalistic prowess is to review the relevant journalism textbooks, stylebooks, and periodicals that may be found in local libraries or in nearby university libraries. If stumped about where to begin, examine the list of publications in Section V of this handbook, or call a journalism department at one the state's colleges or universities and ask to speak with a professor who could recommend reading material. Preferably this college instructor will be someone who is familiar with high school publications and the texts that are used by students and advisers. Also, think about calling other journalism advisers at schools in the area and discuss the current situation with them. Most advisers generally will be sympathetic to your situation and may be able to offer valuable information about journalism teacher-training, in addition to recommending a list of books and periodicals that could be used in class.

Joining Professional Organizations

In addition to such informal contacts with journalism advisers in the immediate area, consider pursuing formal ties with them through local and national organizations. For instance, education cooperatives exist in many states, and these cooperatives sometimes sponsor workshops for journalism teachers and maintain audio-visual material for journalism classes. Local press clubs and local chapters of professional journalism organizations also sponsor journalism workshops and seminars, and media professionals in the area should be able to provide references about what training opportunities these sources offer.

Media professionals and journalism professors also can offer introductions to national journalism associations that offer journalism teacher-training at their conventions and through their publications. While the membership fees are sometimes a bit higher than your budget will allow, at least subscribe to the publications that will offer as much help as possible.

There also may be a state association of high school journalism teachers or at least a high school press association in the area that lends support to inexperienced journalism advisers. By all means make sure to find out about such groups either from the state's Department of Education or from other high school journalism teachers.

If there are no state or regional high school journalism associations to join, at least continue informal contacts with other high school journalism teachers. These advisers can give emotional support and perhaps a crash course in the basics of journalism and publication management.

Obtaining Additional Training and Education

Local media professionals also can offer invaluable assistance on a variety of other levels. For example, if you can afford the time, ask to spend a week or more of the summer vacation (or other vacation time) following local editors and reporters as they complete their daily tasks. Mini-internships of this nature can quickly provide an understanding of a print media operation, which will be important in the scholastic journalism environment. Another thought to consider is spending time with the production people who work in the local media, as they can explain and demonstrate photography, page design, and paste-up techniques. If there is a desire to know a great deal about photography, volunteer your services at a local photography studio in exchange for the training that is desired.

Naturally, if you are an inexperienced yearbook adviser, attending yearbook publication workshops sponsored by yearbook publishing companies is a very good idea. Also, convince the yearbook representative to hold a mini-workshop at the school for you and the staff members. Even if you are not the yearbook adviser, check with the person who is and find out whether the publisher's representative will be holding a workshop at the school or somewhere nearby, and whether the topics to be covered would be of any use to you. Additionally, ask other publication advisers in the area about workshops offered by local colleges and universities, or call the nearby institutions of higher education and inquire about their programs for high school journalists.

Local colleges and universities may also offer journalism classes. Sometimes there are specialty classes such as "directing school publications," but other classes that will help the students' reporting, photography, and design skills are also good. If, for some reason, the taking of regularly offered journalism coursework is impossible, investigate the possibilities offered through continuing education either at local high schools or through area colleges and universities.

Regardless of which avenues you pursue to better your knowledge of journalism, don't overlook the talents the staff members have accumulated during their previous years in high school journalism. Students can teach valuable skills, and it is not disgraceful to tell them you will seek their help while working to overcome minor deficiencies in journalism. Most of the time, students are very understanding of such needs when they are given the chance and when they are treated like adults. Generally, more damage can be done by faking knowledge than by admitting you are temporarily in a difficult position.

Over a relatively short time period, your knowledge of journalism can be expanded so that advising a student publication will be more of a joy than a chore. It may take a good deal of dedication and several weeks attempting to gain ground, but once the initial battles against ignorance have been overcome, the job becomes easier and less stressful.

31

CHAPTER 12

Expanding Instruction Time

Whether the publication you are advising is produced as part of a journalism class or as an extracurricular activity, there will never be enough time to teach all the students what they need to know about reporting, writing, editing, photography, layout, and paste-up. Given all the other responsibilities placed upon a teacher, consider yourself fortunate if most of the tasks associated with the adviser role are completed.

If the publication is part of a journalism class, but not the sole purpose of the class, there will probably be more focus on the academic side of journalism than with publication production. Curriculum guidelines for the class, as approved by the state's Department of Education, may require that in addition to scholastic journalism, there be instruction in journalism history and a survey of mass media as they exist today. If the publication is an extracurricular activity, there is a good chance that there will be even less time for formal instruction. Only those teachers who have newspaper and yearbook production classes on a daily basis will have the luxury of substantial instruction time, but sometimes even these teachers will find themselves wishing for more time to teach the basics.

Create Lesson Plans

To maximize classtime efficiency, pay close attention to the way time is spent with the publication staff. One factor that governs the use of time is the quality of lesson plans. It is very important that the material that is presented to the staff is completed in an effective manner, as the teaching techniques used must be efficient in terms of time and effectiveness.

The organization of class lectures must be well produced and lectures must be kept at a level most of the students can understand, without consistently hovering at the lowest common denominator of comprehension. This is indeed a challenge, and it is one that can be met successfully only after you have obtained a working knowledge of the staff members' capabilities. Thus it is important to spend time getting to know the students before settling in on any one specific teaching methodology.

Schedule Your Academic Life

In addition to creating exceptional lesson plans, carefully plan for the difficult weeks or months that are dotted with heavy amounts of activity and crucial deadlines. During these periods, try to lighten your own workload by assigning reading material to the classes rather than assigning paper work that must be graded. Also, avoid giving in-class examinations to the journalism students, as this will be lost time that could be spent working on the publication. It is perfectly acceptable to balance publication needs with classroom assignments and activities, even when the balancing involves classes unrelated to journalism.

Another way to improve time management is to create calendars and schedules. As with any written aid of this nature, these aids are only helpful if they are checked daily, so place these creations in prominent places and make it a daily habit to post progress notations on them. Encourage the students to do likewise, either on calendars and schedules of their own making or on large, poster-like creations displayed on a classroom bulletin board.

If you have not used this technique before, it may take a month or so to learn how to create realistic schedules. Many teachers, for example, overestimate the number of journalistic tasks that can be done in a certain amount of time. Keeping track of the time that is spent completing various tasks will help you obtain optimal scheduling talents in a minimal number of weeks.

Whatever type of calendar or schedule that is attempted and decided upon, make sure to build in some "lost days." These are days in which absolutely nothing is accomplished, and they occur because of bad weather, previously unscheduled school assemblies, field trips, bad mental attitudes, fire drills, and a variety of other interruptions. A good rule of thumb is to embed in the schedule about one lost day for every two weeks. If a scheduled lost day does not have to be used during a certain time period, use this time to catch up on lessons or to reward the staff for conscientiously working to meet deadlines.

Do not inform the staff members there are hidden lost days in any schedule that is created for them to follow. If the students know there are "lost days", they will intentionally take advantage of them. There is no reason for the staff members to be made aware of this technique, and they should be encouraged to beat whatever deadline is posted.

Set Priorities

When planning a calendar or other type of schedule, setting priorities will be mandatory because all of the necessary material can not be covered at once. This may be frustrating because the situation may seem to dictate that everything needs to be taught first. While this may be a realistic assessment, it isn't possible to meet such a need, and there will have to be a decision as to the most useful order for covering subjects the staff will find helpful.

In addition to setting priorities for lessons to be covered, make sure to set priorities for the types of publication-related tasks you are willing to do. Because time is limited, the need to delegate some degree of responsibility to members of the staff or members of the school types of boundaries most useful to advisers are those that define the tasks which actually can be done and those that define a time frame for completing such tasks. Advisers, therefore, must gain an understanding of how much they can do and how long it will take them to do it. When accurate answers to these questions are determined, it is much easier for advisers to operate successfully within the alloted instruction time available to them.

New advisers must be more careful than experienced advisers in attempting to decide the number of tasks that can be done. This is true because inexperienced advisers generally underestimate the amount of time their publication responsibilities will take. Thus new advisers need to be cautious about volunteering for or otherwise accepting additional school-related duties such as sponsoring clubs and organizations or serving on committees that monitor other extracurricular sports and social activities.

administration may be required. This topic also was touched upon in Chapter 10, but it is worth reiterating in this context as it can do much more than make your job more pleasant; it also can make the difference between a job that is manageable and a job that is impossible. Don't be afraid to let go of some control over the operation of the publication. After all, students learn by assuming responsibility, and if their progress is monitored, disasters can easily be avoided.

Set Reasonable Goals

Related to the idea of organizing tasks into a reasonable order of importance is the idea of placing boundaries on the tasks that have been so carefully ordered. The two

High school journalism advisers, more than other school employees, need to say no to many of the other tasks administrators will offer to them. This is not to suggest that any extra curricular activities that are offered by school administrators should be declined, but there should be careful consideration as to accepting what seems to be the "normal" load for your colleagues. Relatively speaking, the job as adviser will take more time to complete than seemingly comparable tasks will take your colleagues to complete. That is because there are no comparable tasks that fellow colleagues have to complete.

In deciding just how many tasks will be accepted, make a decision concerning just how long it will take to accomplish these tasks. Again, if you are a new adviser, the decision-making process will probably be difficult because accurate judgment comes with experience. One of the best steps that can be taken to help yourself with this problem is to find out about the schedules maintained by current or former advisers in the local area. This can be achieved through personal contacts with them or through contacts with administrators (or their secretaries) at your school and at other local schools.

When conversing with other advisers, do not be afraid to ask for specific details concerning time requirements for publication-related tasks. For example, ask them how much out-of-class time they spend on the publication, and ask them why they must do so. Many will tell you that their out-of-class time varies from week to week, depending on deadlines and other factors, but most will explain that advising takes more time than any other academic or extracurricular task they have experienced. Also, ask them if they are exempt from other extracurricular duties that their colleagues are more or less forced to do. In some schools, advisers do not have lunchroom duty or study hall duty.

Ultimately, there will be a need to make decisions about the number of goals to be pursued and about the amount of time that must be spent to reach these goals. Make these important decisions early in the year and stick to them if at all possible. Remember, these decisions can be adjusted if they become unreasonable.

Take Preventive Measures

When becoming a publication adviser, it will be very useful to understand time management techniques so that the amount of time you and the staff members spend inefficiently will decrease over time. If you are not well read in this field, make a serious effort to read several books about time management. As you comprehend the theories and techniques concerning time management, attempt to apply them to the high school environment and to any specific publication situation. Of course, some of the methods suggested in the reading have to be adapted to fit the high school environment, but the principles that were discovered in the readings should hold true for any leadership position, including that of a publication adviser.

Additionally, give consideration to consulting with other publication advisers in the area to find out the successful techniques they have used. If there is a college or university nearby, consult with the business or management professors who specialize in time management. If nothing else, these people should be able to recommend relevant readings.

Another preventive measure that can be taken is to lobby for separate journalism production classes, if they are not already scheduled. There is no good reason to be forced to do publication advising within the confines of a journalism class in which basic journalism techniques are taught along with journalism history and other topics related to mass media. It is even more ridiculous for the school administration to expect you to advise a student newspaper or yearbook that is produced as an extracurricular activity. A good journalism program would include at least one daily class to produce a publication. If there isn't one, no school administrator will provide one unless there is enough lobbying for and discussion about such a change.

When lobbying for a separate laboratory class, compare the situation to other high school journalism programs in the area, obtain support from local media professionals and university professors, and obtain supporting information from regional and national scholastic journalism organizations. If journalism is recognized as a language art by your state's Department of Education, point out that in order to teach the subject matter adequately, there is a need for two classes; one class to teach journalistic writing principles and another class to conduct the activities associated with a student publication. Perhaps comparing the quality of the school's publications to the quality of publications from area schools that have publication laboratories will also support your argument.

The idea of adding journalism classes to the school's schedule may not be well received by the administration or school board, and quick decisions and actions in this area should not be expected. Pursue this goal relentlessly, however, as everyone concerned will be better off when it is achieved.

Whatever steps that are taken to offset the lack of instruction time as a publication adviser, there still won't be enough time in the day. This is to be expected, but if the situation does improve a little bit each month, there is a good chance for survival. Overall, it is most important that you recognize ways to alleviate the problem and implement the most available solutions as soon as possible.

CHAPTER 13

Selecting Staff Members the Right Way

The amount of authority advisers have to select staff members for the newspaper or yearbook operation varies from school to school. Some advisers have complete authority to accept and reject students who apply to be staff members, while other advisers must accept anyone who either registers for journalism credit or who volunteers to work on the staff.

Regardless of the amount of authority that is given to the adviser, there are three steps that advisers can take to ensure that there are competent people in the editorial leadership positions on the staff: recruit vigorously, test thoroughly, and check background completely.

Recruit Vigorously

To obtain a reasonable number of staff members who are talented in a variety of areas, talk to as many "select" students as possible. For example, visit honors English classes to recruit writers and editors, art classes to recruit students with layout and design skills, photography classes to recruit competent photographers, and business classes to recruit typists, office managers, and advertising managers. For each class visited, present a five-minute presentation about the publication program and the opportunities specific to the interests of the students being addressed. Speak well of the publication, and balance the description of the demanding work with a list of extra rewards that staff members receive.

Also think about asking fellow colleagues to recommend students whom they think will be able to do exceptional work as members of a publication staff. It would be natural to ask teachers whose teaching specialties coincide with your needs, and when they provide the information requested, follow up on it as soon as possible. Individual conferences with prospective staff members are generally much more effective than form letters that encourage students to apply for staff positions.

Additionally, ask current staff members to encourage their responsible and talented friends to apply for staff positions. While frequent visits to classes can be helpful in recruiting, friend-to-friend pressure can be even more effective. The only drawback to asking students to encourage their friends to apply is that sometimes a staff member's judgment of responsibility and talent differs from your own. This is one reason why thorough testing of prospective applicants is strongly advised.

Test Thoroughly

Although advisers always attempt to interest only the best students in becoming newspaper or yearbook staff members, they invariably attract students whose abilities range from excellent to nonexistent. Therefore, when sufficient interest has been generated in the student publication staff positions, it is necessary to weed out those students who show no real talent for or interest in doing what will be required of them. Several methods may be used to achieve this goal.

One method is to require all applicants to fill out application forms. In some way or another, questions on the form should extract crucial information that will allow you to make fairly accurate judgments about the applicants.

Useful information to obtain would concern what journalism experience, relevant classes, or other relevant experience the applicant has, what grades the applicant has earned in relevant classes, what position the applicant is applying for, and exactly what the applicant plans to do for the publication. Also, try to determine how much time per week the applicant plans to spend on the publication, whether or not the applicant has a vehicle (especially if advertising sales are involved), and what extracurricular activities the applicant pursues. Extracurricular activities should include employment at school and after school. Finally, to determine why the applicant wants to be a staff member, require an essay that addresses this question.

After the applicants have completed the first "tests" (i.e., filling out applications and demonstrating the dedication that publication work requires), require them to complete some kind of formal test in writing, editing, spelling, page design, or photography. Many of the original applicants won't bother to return the application form, so in the second stage of the application process, you will be dealing with a smaller number of students than at the first stage of the process. The formal test is also a good technique to use in situations where the adviser doesn't have control over enrollment in publication activities, e.g., at schools in which anyone can sign up, even over the protests of the adviser.

When it isn't practical to give formal tests in areas such as page design or photography, ask to see samples of applicants' work. Often, such samples allow an easier decision to be made about the applicants' abilities.

If the situation requires you to accept all students who either sign up for journalism or volunteer to work on the school publication, make good use of the application and formal test procedures to help determine which students should be placed in positions of responsibility. Obviously, pay close attention for signs of talent and dedication when filling these positions, but also check on student availability for out-of-class activities.

Check Background Completely

No matter what students put on their applications, always check to see if the information is correct. In terms of an applicant's academic life, both past and present grade point average and coursework can easily be checked. It is important for students who have been placed in

35

positions of responsibility to have more than minimal grade point averages, as the time they will need to spend on the publication may consume some of the study time required to do at least average work in their other classes. Additionally, make sure that the students who are editors, do not have class schedules which overburden them with difficult, time-consuming classes.

In terms of abilities, check with former teachers to see exactly how the applicant has acted in class, and ask colleagues how they would evaluate the applicant in terms of ability to function as a publication staff member. Another way to check an applicant's abilities would be to ask for evaluations from peers who either know them well or have worked with them in other situations. Be selective about the peer evaluators you choose to rely upon, as some students are neither reliable enough nor mature enough to provide the sensitive information you need. Letters of recommendation from adults who have previously worked with the applicant could also be accepted

Additionally, when applicants list extracurricular activities on their applications, find out from the sponsors of those activities exactly how much time will be required of the students involved in them. Some students have a tendency to attempt more than they have time to do, and you don't want to be in the position of having to replace a key staff member who has decided to devote less time to the publication staff in order to meet other obligations. Finally, verify with the applicants the amount of time they will spend at off-campus jobs. Students who work just a few hours per week in August or September may be asked to increase their hours during holiday seasons, which also may be crucial deadline seasons for the publication.

Once the recruitment, testing, and background checking is finalized for all of the applicants, you should have an excellent grasp of each student's abilities and an accurate judgment about where each student might be placed on the publication staff. Even if all of the applicants have to be accepted, creating a workable hierarchy should be a fairly easy task. All that remains are the personal interviews with each of the accepted applicants who have been designated publication editors. Inform them of the decision and obtain their advice concerning the rest of the students on the staff. The latter activity should not be overlooked because it serves to build your relationship with your editors.

Sample Staff Application

Name_____

Address_____

Phone number_____

Class standing (circle one): FR SO JR SR

Current grade point average_____

Position desired_____

In an essay on a separate page, explain why you desire this position and exactly what you plan to do for this publication.

Journalism experience_____
_____

Previous journalism classes (include grades earned)_____
_____

Current journalism classes_____

Other classes in which you are enrolled _____
_____
_____

Relevant experience_____

Number of hours per week you can devote to this publication_____

Other school, church, or community activities in which you participate_____
_____

If you are employed, list place(s) of employment, workdays, and number of hours per week you work at your job(s)_____
_____

Do you have a vehicle or access to a vehicle? (circle one)

yes no

CHAPTER 14

Overcoming Problems Generated by Predecessors

There are generally three major problems generated by previous publications advisers, and they involve either personal or financial considerations. When taking over an advising position from a teacher who has held it for some time, one problem that will be encountered concerns an established method of doing things; a second problem involves residual "clinging" behavior that is mutually shared by the former adviser and the current staff. A third problem, often associated with replacement of a short-term teacher, is that there might be a budget deficit which must be dealt with during the first year of advising.

Fighting Tradition

One of the first tasks, when taking over a publication from a predecessor of long-standing tenure, is to find out how the operation was run by that person. Preferably, you will be able to meet with this person and fully discuss the publication, its staff, and the intricacies of the former adviser's role. If certain circumstances make such a meeting impossible, at least write or call the adviser who is departing to ascertain as much relevant information as possible.

Before the start of the school year, find out as much as possible about the publication operation you are going to be advising. This information will be a beneficial in determining how much your method of advising differs from the predecessor's techniques. If the differences are vast, discuss with the administration and the staff the changes that are desired. To reduce potential conflict, provide clear support for such changes.

Often, the resistance to change can be overcome without having to fight a long series of disruptive battles, by settling for gradual change rather than immediate, total change. This will be particularly true concerning changes in the content of the publication, the way the publication looks, or the amount of freedom the staff members will have in doing their jobs. While knowing that the content is too immature, that the layouts violate every existing rule of design, or that the students are too used to being told exactly what to do, don't expect sweeping changes to be readily accepted by all concerned.

If a former adviser has for years encouraged such content and makeup, and has ruled the staff with the proverbial iron hand, be satisfied if being able to convince only the administrators to support your ideas for change. After convincing the school administration to support these changes, turn your attention to the first-year staff members and convince them that these changes are for the betterment of the publication. Consider yourself lucky if one or two second- or third-year staff members accept some of these new ideas. Eventually, you will outlast tradition.

The struggle for change will be more successful if support for it can be obtained from the previous adviser. If this adviser is still employed in the school district, ask this person to show support for these changes by telling the staff members they should not expect a carbon copy of past advisers. Of course, if you find out before the school year ends that you will be assuming the responsibilities of a publication adviser, try to arrange a chat with the current adviser and ask to be introduced to the publication staff. Prepare a brief, positive statement about ideas and plans for making next year's operation the best it can possibly be.

After assuming this new position, talk with the staff members about their former adviser, and clear the air of any hostility toward you, if any exists. Additionally, take this opportunity to justify the new method of operation, explaining the advantages of the ideas for change. Such discussions should help pave the way for change.

This is also a good time to make it clear to the students that they should come to you for advice and counsel, rather than seeking out the former adviser. When the former adviser remains in the school, some seasoned staff members will continue to use that person as a sounding board for their publication ideas. If this problem arises, diplomatically tell the former adviser that such conduct is not appreciated and ask that these advice-seekers be sent back to you for advice. Such support is vital to your survival as an effective adviser, and it is needed to ensure stability regardless of how delicate the situation is.

Making Up A Deficit

When taking the place of an inexperienced adviser, especially if a yearbook is involved, an inherited deficit may require immediate attention. When encountering this problem, increasing revenue and decreasing costs are the two ways to solve the problem.

Ways to increase revenue are discussed in Chapter 20, which concentrates on funding problems in general; but cost-cutting steps that can significantly reduce the deficit also may be taken.

One such step is to reduce the number of pages in the newspaper or yearbook, especially if there is very little advertising to support the publication. In commercial newspaper operations, for example, the amount of advertising governs the number of pages each issue contains. If the three-to-one advertising-to-news ratio of commercial papers cannot be matched, do not allow the amount of news to govern the size of the paper. Instead, require the editors to choose wisely among the available editorial copy. Similarly, to reduce the number of pages contained in the yearbook, discuss with the editors the sections that could be reduced and the spreads that could be left out.

Another option to consider is reducing the number of newspaper issues that the staff distributes within the academic school year. This can be done without losing opportunities to actually produce newspaper copy, as you can supply an enclosed school bulletin board or showcase with weekly stories produced by the staff. The display area should have a section clearly labeled "fresh copy" or "new stories," so whenever a staff member produces a fresh story, it can be placed in a spot where it will receive attention.

Another deficit-reducing step is to eliminate the frills in the publication. For example, in terms of pure cost, color in yearbooks is very expensive, and thus consideration should be given to substituting some spot color throughout a few signatures (four-page, eight-page, or sixteen-page spreads) for the full-color pictures that would normally be run. Spot color means using one primary color (blue, red, yellow) or one mixed color, on designated pages. The yearbook representative should be able to describe all of the variations available with spot color, and with proper screens, they can make a yearbook look almost as good as it would look with full color. In fact, using screens with only the black ink in the publication can produce some superior visual results. This is true for newspaper production as well.

Other frills that could be eliminated include fancy covers and fancy end sheets (for yearbooks), and graphics or other artwork that is expensive either to produce or reproduce (for both newspapers and yearbooks). Obtaining cost estimates for these types of frills should be able to provide enough information for you to decide whether or not the expense is justified. If there are questions concerning savings on production costs, ask for some help from either a printing representative or someone who operates a local printing business. Do not guess at this crucial information, for a bad guess can cost a great deal of money. Printing experts can also offer advice about the type of paper being used for the publication, and this is valuable because some types of paper cost much less than other types.

If the newspaper contains pictures, there can be a way to save revenue according to the way the staff groups the pictures for the company that prepares them for printing. Check with the printer to see what costs the most and what costs the least, in terms of picture preparation. Discussing similar options with the yearbook representative would also be a good idea.

Also, a considerable amount of money often is wasted by students in the preparation of their copy. Careless errors, which require typesetting corrections or entire page design changes, can be exceedingly costly. Additionally, the way in which editorial copy is sent to off-campus typesetters can make a significant difference in cost. Grouping all the copy requiring the same type style and column width sometimes can result in big savings.

With a little maneuvering, there also may be a chance of an educator's discount from some of the people who do business with the publication. Examples of this would be obtaining film at cost from the yearbook photographer or obtaining cost breaks (usually 10 percent) from businesses that supply the staff with graphics arts materials. In states that honor tax identification numbers, retailers will not charge a sales tax on items that are purchased, if the school has such a number. Check with school administrators to see if this is true for your situation.

While there is no one "best way" to deal with problems generated by the previous adviser, a variety of approaches may be used to alleviate the indignities that will be encountered when entering an ongoing school publications operation. To paraphrase a well-known historical figure, all of the approaches will work some of the time, some of the approaches will work all of the time, but not all of the approaches will work all of the time. Do not despair when an approach does not work; merely move on to the next one and hope for the best.

CHAPTER 15

Providing and Accepting Criticism Gracefully

Chapter 8 dealt with students' inability to accept criticism and several techniques that can help staff members overcome this problem were discussed. This included forewarning the students that criticism is a necessary and accepted aspect of journalism, inviting a professional journalist to the school to critique the staff members' work, holding group critique sessions so that students can find their own errors, and providing certain types of criticism in private meetings with individual staff members.

Although this chapter contains suggestions that complement the material discussed previously, the approach is different. Here, one focus is on the adviser's problems as a provider of criticism, and one focus is on the adviser's problems as a recipient of criticism.

Providing Criticism

In general, teachers are paid to criticize. Every time they grade student work of any nature, they are in fact critiquing that work. The adviser's duties are no different from a teacher's duties in other classes, whether or not staff members are obtaining credit for their work. Almost all of the staff members need help to improve their journalistic efforts, and to achieve this goal, constructive criticism must be applied to their journalistic writing.

It is not unusual for journalism advisers to be more willing to criticize academic work than publications work. One reason for this is that advisers often see publications work as being less crucial than other class assignments. This is a false impression. As an adviser, an attitude must be developed that student publications really matter, regardless of what school administrators, fellow colleagues, and students believe. Student publications really do matter because they represent one of the few avenues through which high school students can practice their citizenship and gain practical experience in the language skills and social skills they will use throughout their lives.

When you are comfortable with this attitude, the next task is to overcome any reluctance to provide criticism at the individual or group level. While successful advisers are not shy about providing constructive criticism, they are aggressive without being abrasive. Remember, if only unoffensive errors are pointed out, then the publication will most likely lack any hint of professionalism, and the students will be wasting much of the time they spend on their work.

Returning to the concept of criticism, please note that early in the year there is a need to define for the students the difference between "constructive" and "destructive" criticism. Explain to them that the intent is to criticize a product rather than a person, and that the criticism being offered will not be vindictive in nature. Also, tell them that the goal of the criticism is to improve both their work as individuals and the finished product as a whole.

Certainly, there will be a need to balance criticism with praise. Just as it was suggested in Chapter 8 that during group critique sessions you encourage staff members to provide each other with both criticism and praise, you also must give considerable positive reinforcement to the staff members. Be careful not to create an image as someone who always finds fault with the staff members' work.

To help balance the criticism with praise, keep meticulous records concerning the progress that staff members make. Good records will help determine the ways in which work is improving, and it will also be beneficial in grading staff members (if grading is required) and in justifying the removal of dysfunctional students from the staff. Additionally, records that are kept will help the consistency of the praise and criticism that is given, and that, too, is important.

If you have the luxury of serving as adviser for more than one year, there will be the chance of using contest critiques to back up the criticism that is provided. Be sure to enter the students' publications in at least one contest that offers a total critique of their entire yearbook and/or newspaper. Generally, professionals will be involved in such contests, and these professionals will complete a form that contains a point-by-point evaluation of the students' publication. When this form is returned to the school, share it with the students so they will see how imperfect they are. The chances are good that this report will then back up your role as a reviewer of the students' work.

Finally, two other aspects of providing criticism must be considered. First, be sure not to play favorites. In spite of the fact that there will be some excellent students in the class, do not use their work as the obvious standard by which to measure the work of others. Conversely, do not consistently use the work of the poorest students as public examples of incompetence, even though these students frequently provide ample material for seminars that could be titled, "What not to do in journalism."

Second, and perhaps most important of all the ideas presented so far in this chapter, is the idea that great strides should be taken to listen to what the students have to say. Remember, they are not professionals, and often they have what seems like perfectly acceptable reasons for doing what they do. If you listen to them before criticizing their work, a pleasant relationship with the staff will be built. This is true because the staff members will learn that you care about what they think, and it will allow you to better understand how they think. With this in mind, the criticism that is offered will be better shaped and easily understood.

Accepting Criticism

Publication staff members are not the only people who will receive criticism for their work. You, as the adviser, will find that everyone is a critic. Due to this, be prepared to expect criticism from the school administration, fellow colleagues, parents, and students who are not on staff.

As a preventive measure, educate these potential critics in terms of how the journalistic process works. This particularly concerns the teachers and coaches who will want coverage for the organization or group events they sponsor. To avoid the criticism that the staff did not adequately cover something, contact these people early in the year, explain to them the requirements they must meet to obtain coverage (notification deadlines, types of coverage available), and provide them with a detailed form to complete concerning the events they want covered (dates, places, rosters, significance of events, and other pertinent information). Include in this category any person who is likely to request coverage or complain that inadequate coverage was provided. If you are new to the school, some concentrated scouting may have to be done during the first few weeks of school, but the dividends are worth the time invested.

Another preventive measure that can be considered is to conduct tours of the journalism operation. Generally, if outsiders realize how difficult it is to put together a publication, they will make extra efforts to meet deadlines well in advance. They may also be more likely to give very specific information about the type of coverage they desire. Knowing that the process is complex and open to error at a variety of stages often serves to motivate outsiders to be more mindful of the importance their actions play in preventing problems.

In addition to being criticized for providing too little coverage, the publication may also be criticized for giving too much coverage to certain groups or students. To help avoid this criticism, post a "leper list" in a prominent spot on the publication's bulletin board, and on it require the students to keep track of people who already have appeared in the publication two or three times. Then, when the staff chooses future pictures to include, ask them to check the "leper list" to see if they are violating the rule of distributed publicity, i.e., spreading coverage among as many of the school population as possible. This rule applies to all forms of the student press, and it should be regularly enforced.

When criticism is directed at the publication, as it invariably will, stay calm and be patient. It will not help to become hostile, because this only causes ill will between you and the people you must deal with as long as you stay in the school district. To help the situation, disarm these critics by inquiring about their reaction to the publication as a whole. Often, they will have good comments to make in addition to their criticisms, and by diverting their attention, this encounter will seem more reasonable.

To show that there is general interest in their criticisms, provide these critics with a detailed form to complete. The form should allow them to categorize their criticisms and to suggest ways in which coverage could be improved. Assure them that the information they are giving will be shared with the staff. Even if these critics decline to complete such forms, make it a habit to share with the staff members the criticisms that are received from external sources.

When criticisms from outside sources are received by the publication, serve as a mature example for the staff members to follow. Show the students that this type of criticism can be accepted and accepted without a showing of ill will, even if the criticism is not justified. If it is valid, work with the staff to correct the problem. Be sure to apply the principles to all events similar to those from which the criticism originated.

Providing and accepting criticism can be a terribly taxing experience, at least from a psychological standpoint, and there has to be a concerted effort to rise above the personal aspects of the processes involved. Dealing with criticism is a natural part of your role, and whether you provide it or receive it, the handling of it is an important factor in the relationships with those who surround you.

CHAPTER 16
Avoiding Taking Over

One of the most dangerous problems that advisers must confront involves their participation in the publication process. The problem arises almost invariably when staff members fall behind in their work and fail to meet critical deadlines, for in these circumstances it is natural for advisers to step in with assistance.

While giving help to the staff is easy to justify, two equally unsatisfactory results occur when advisers become overly involved in their work: too much precious time is spent doing what an adviser shouldn't have to do, and this places the adviser in an editorial role. Concerning the first matter, most advisers will soon discover that there is not enough time in the day to do what is required, and adding the students' tasks to their schedules will make daily life miserable. Concerning the second matter, advisers who work for public school systems are legally considered to be arms of the state, and they should not be working on student publications. Claims of censorship may be raised when advisers take an active role in the editorial process, no matter how innocent the actions are.

While recent U.S. Supreme Court decisions allow public schools more control over student publications produced in a journalism laboratory setting, censorship still causes two problems. First, it undermines basic journalistic principles and thus serves as a poor role model. Second, charges of censorship create bad publicity for the program, school, and the school district.

There is no question that serious thought must be given to adviser actions that help the staff. To help clarify the thought process and develop personal guidelines, define the adviser role in advance and take precautions based upon that definition.

Define Your Role

There are at least three times when the definition of an adviser is needed The first time occurs when advisers accept the position, for they must decide what role they play in that position. It is necessary to decide the boundaries of participation long before standing in front of the staff to welcome them back to school in the fall. Have a game plan in mind, know how much you are willing to do to save a weak staff from their incompetence, and also give consideration to the consequences of these decisions. How much criticism are you willing to take from outsiders if you don't step in when the staff doesn't deliver?

To help determine these advisory boundaries, discuss the position with other advisers or journalism professors in the region. These people should be able to provide both idealistic and realistic guidelines. Also, check with the former adviser at the school to find out what the staff members might be expecting in terms of participation. Their expectations could be a major factor in the approach used when discussing the adviser role with them.

The second time a role definition is needed also comes before the beginning of school. At some point, there needs to be an explanation to your supervisors as to just how much you are willing to do in the role as adviser. This is necessary so no one is surprised at the actions taken during the production process. For example, if the game plan calls for the newspaper staff to miss a deadline in order to teach them a lesson, make sure to gain administrative support for that action before it happens.

Before approaching school supervisors, find out about the past relationships and expectations the administration has had concerning student publications. Again, former advisers can be very helpful in providing this information; students and colleagues also are good sources of such information.

The third time the adviser definition is needed is during the first week of school, when you discuss it with the staff. During this meeting, make the definition crystal clear, but scaring the staff into thinking you will be no help at all is counter-productive. As delicately as possible, explain the legal and practical aspects of the adviser's role, and make clear to the staff that they will be denied their educational experience if they do not complete a significant amount of work themselves.

If you have a good grasp of the definition of an adviser, it will be no problem explaining this role to others, and it can be done without offending any audience. Certainly, there may be occasions to expand the definition of this role, as circumstances permit, but it is better to begin with a narrow definition than with an a broad, vague explanation.

Take Precautions

Defining the role of the adviser will enable you to ensure success in maintaining that role. When you and others in the school clearly understand the adviser's role, a certain set of mutual expectations develops. This is very useful because it reduces the amount of conflict that might occur in the publication environment. Of course, the definition of the role as adviser should complement other steps that have been taken to guarantee overall staff success, as discussed in previous chapters, e.g., choosing capable staff members and arranging relevant training.

When the staff members realize how involved you are willing to become in day-to-day operations, they will more readily accept the precautionary steps taken to keep the adviser from crossing into staff members' territory. For example, the students will allow the delegation of authority and should expect evaluation of their independent work with some form of grade. Additionally, they will accept it as normal procedure to be referred to various references for answers to their questions about spelling, grammar, or writing style, and soon they will learn to seek assistance in these areas only as a last resort. Searching for their own errors after publication will also become routine.

Another precautionary step that can be taken during production time is to prevent the students from drawing you into the activity. Achieve this by doing busy work, along with other tasks, so staff members may not be able to interrupt. Creating periods of "dead time," which are clearly designated as times when students may not bother you, may work well with staff members who are mature enough to understand these motives. "Dead time" is a bit more extreme than merely working intently at your desk while the staff works on the publication, but sometimes it is necessary to create the types of barriers that force students to be independent.

Whatever steps you take to avoid becoming the main force behind the students' publication, be prepared to be flexible. Good advisers, no matter how strict they are, will sometimes cross their boundaries of participation because the advantages of doing so will far outweigh the disadvantages of holding fast to an arbitrary philosophy.

If you do violate the stated philosophy, be sure to explain to the students why this decision was made, making it clear that such action will not be a common occurrence. Discussions of this nature may lead to more respect and a better understanding from the staff.

CHAPTER 17

Grading Guidelines Made Reasonable

The process of assigning grades for work on a publication staff often perplexes advisers, especially when the publication is not produced in conjunction with a journalism class. When the student newspaper or yearbook is produced as an extracurricular activity, no grades may be necessary, but some form of periodic evaluation may serve to improve the overall operation. For example, identifying and ranking the capabilities of staff members allows the adviser and editors to justify staff assignments and avoid a variety of small disasters.

As an adviser, the evaluation and grading process can be broken into two distinctively different areas. The first area involves evaluation planning, which concerns the steps taken in developing the grading system. The second area concerns all that you do during the grading process.

Evaluation Planning

If you have never advised a student publication, it would be useful to contact other advisers in the area and ask them about their evaluation and grading procedures. This information should provide some ideas upon which to base your own grading system. Some advisers base staff members' grades on a variety of factors, including skills competency, number of assignments completed, attendance at staff meetings, cooperation with others, and overall participation.

If there is some previous student publication advising in your background, then you realize the skill needed to develop an evaluation system, and this experience can be used to create a grading formula. Going over the grading formula with former students may yield some new ideas from them that can be incorporated into the current grading process. If it is possible to meet with the current editorial staff before the beginning of school, ask them for suggestions and use their ideas if they can be worked into the system.

After obtaining as much information as possible from the various sources that have been contacted, create written guidelines that clearly define the grading policy. The guidelines should be as specific as possible, but they also should leave some room for adjustment. In other words, reserve the right to raise or lower grades according to intangibles such as attitude and cooperation.

Once the evaluation guidelines have been created, share these guidelines with administrators at the school. Do more than merely send copies of the guidelines to them; request a meeting at which any questions can be answered. It's a good idea to make administrators aware of your advising plans, and it is helpful to obtain their support for a grading system that may eliminate dysfunctional staff members.

When the administrators agree to these guidelines, incorporate them into the publication's stylebook and point them out to staff members as soon as possible. Once you have met with the staff and discussed grading procedures with them, send copies of the grading guidelines to the staff members' parents. If a contract system is being used, as discussed in Chapter 3, it would be good to include the grading guidelines with the contract that the parents are asked to sign at the beginning of the year.

By sharing grading guidelines with administrators, students, and parents, most chances of any misunderstandings are eliminated. Additionally, you have created the impression that publication production is more than a simple activity which can be taken lightly.

The Grading Process

After designing the grading system, make sure to take steps that will ensure its success. It is simply not acceptable to proceed "by the seat of your pants" and hope for the best.

One step to take is to create evaluation sheets, which should be completed periodically for each staff member. These sheets should provide places for comments on each person's progress in all of the areas that have been designated in the grading guidelines. The sheets should be dated and discussed with each staff member on a monthly basis, if not more frequently. File these sheets after a private discussion with each staff member and have each student sign the report.

To complete the evaluation sheets accurately, you'll need to keep meticulous records of student work. This requires building a good working relationship with the editors and perhaps paying consistently closer attention to individuals than you might ordinarily pay to students in your other classes. If a merit-demerit system is chosen in conjunction with the grading process, keep good track of the relevant information on which the merits and demerits are based. Many advisers find that such systems are undesirable because they are complicated, unnecessary, and open to abuse.

Quizzes and tests that cover spelling, style, and technique are other sources of information that ultimately may be incorporated into a final grade. For example, require the staff members to learn 50-100 of the most frequently misspelled words, as this will help them in a variety of ways. Another quiz can test the staff members' working knowledge of the publication's style, especially if an up-to-date style book has been created for the students to follow. Finally, all staff members should be required to have a working knowledge of the techniques involved in their areas of specialization on the publication, e.g., writing and editing, photography, and design and layout. Occasional attempts to measure competence in these areas are not unreasonable.

To call attention to individual progress, require the

students to keep up with their grades in ways other than discussing them with you during periodic evaluations. One way to do this is to require the staff members to keep track of their publication work, by preparing a daily list of all the relevant tasks they have contributed to or completed. At the end of each week, require that staff members provide a record of their work, which you should place in their folders along with the periodic evaluation forms. When staff members consistently have little evidence that they are doing something for the publication, be sure to discuss this with them during their individual evaluation meetings.

Just prior to the time that grades have to be turned in for the staff members, ask them to write self-evaluations. Require them to include in these evaluations the grades they would assign to themselves and the justifications for such grades. This process allows the staff members an opportunity to analyze their contributions to the publication and an opportunity to explain why they should receive higher grades than you might think they deserve.

Although the information obtained through this exercise may not cause a change in an evaluation of a particular student, it may serve another more important purpose. Sometimes, evaluations of this nature are enlightening because they provide advisers with insights about the way their students see the world of journalism. From a teaching standpoint, that information can be priceless.

Even when the most perfect grading system has been developed, there may be a need for adjustment now and then, either for an entire group or on a case-by-case basis. Don't worry about minor adjustments, for small changes are not important. What is important is that a visible evaluation system has been created which will refute any charges of favoritism in grading and allow you to justify any personnel decisions that need to be made.

CHAPTER 18
Retracing Old Ground the Painless Way

The problem of retracing old ground is as much a student problem as it is an adviser problem, but because the adviser has more control over the situation than do staff members, this chapter has been placed in this section of the handbook. Retracing old ground refers to the need for repetition of training. Early in the school year, the adviser often is expected to teach basic journalistic skills to staff members. According to some sequential plan, students practice simple skills before they tackle the more complicated ones.

During the course of the school year, as substance becomes more important to students than form, advisers sometimes find that the staff members' work violates the basic rules discussed early in the semester. This becomes evident, for example, when the leads of otherwise well-done stories are buried in the middle of these stories, or when the common rules of page design are lost to ungoverned experimentation.

If the staff members fall victim to their enthusiasm, at least to the extent that they begin to produce work which shows deviation from an acceptable norm, it is the responsibility of the adviser to guide them gently back toward the correct path. Definitely, do not stifle their creativity, but at the same time make sure they adhere to the principles upon which good writing, photography, and design are based.

Frequently, when making notes of staff members' errors, the students will accept these comments without resentment. Sometimes, however, when group exercises are used to review past training, the students will complain that they've done this before and they don't need to do it again. This is where the real problem arises.

To avoid the complaints that are likely to accompany the "retraining" exercises, a few simple precautionary steps can be taken. First, in the original discussions of basic skills, plant the idea in staff members' minds that periodic review of these skills will take place on an ongoing basis. You might note that professionals often take refresher courses in their areas of specialization, and thus it is not a disgrace to take part in review procedures of this nature.

Explain to the staff members that as they learn more about journalism, it will be natural for them to shift their focus from the more elementary ideas to the more complex issues. Explain that this is being done to develop their skills, but that such growth cannot be accomplished at the expense of ignoring basic guidelines. If the students expect periodic retraining, they will not resent it every time it is introduced.

Second, whenever a retraining exercise is scheduled, refer to it in a way that avoids the appearance of punishment. Instead, it should have the ring of skills enhancement to it. For example, call it a "professional adjustment," which has the connotation that the exercise will help to make the students work less amateurish. It will be obvious to the staff members, whatever you call it, that they will be retracing old ground, but if it is presented in a friendly manner, the staff will develop a good attitude about the process.

Third, when conducting a review session, use material that is of interest to the students. There is nothing more boring for them than to work with exercises which have little relevance to their world. As topics for the exercises, use local or state news that the students might reasonably be expected to know about. Also, incorporate their names into the exercises, as they will be used to writing about students and because use of their names will make the exercises seem less obscure to them.

Finally, make the experience as much fun as possible. An idea might be to divide the staff into teams, and on an individual or group basis, reward the best team at the end of the session. For example, if you are reviewing style, hold a contest similar to a spelling bee, rewarding each individual for a correct answer. Another idea is to provide worksheets and then score each team's efforts, rewarding the team with the best average score. Rewards could be anything from individual pieces of food (nuts, fruit, or candy) to exemptions from future assignments.

However the retraining session is conducted, do not worry that too much time is being spent teaching the basic skills that the staff members need to know. The students will use these skills throughout their journalistic careers and in many nonjournalistic aspects of their lives. They really cannot practice these skills enough, so don't let a little opposition to "professional adjustment" be a deterrent to periodically retracing old ground.

SECTION III

SOLVING PROBLEMS ASSOCIATED WITH ADMINISTRATORS

CHAPTER 19

Building Support, Understanding and Expectations

Although some high school principals and superintendents treat high school journalism as the important learning experience that it should be, it is not uncommon for administrators to view high school journalism as either a potential embarrassment or a frivolous activity that must be tolerated because of tradition. This is true, in part, because administrators do not understand the journalistic process and because they have low expectations of high school journalism. Consequently, they often do not lend financial or moral support to journalism programs.

Unfortunately, in many school systems, journalism really is a frivolous activity, resulting in poorly produced student newspapers and yearbooks; however, there is no good reason why students must continue to produce inferior publications. In the role as adviser, through persistent communication and action, you can improve administrative understanding of the journalistic process and thereby teach administrators to have higher expectations about student journalism. In turn, they can be convinced to support the school's journalism program with more than minimal funding and cooperation. This may need to be pursued, however, for what may turn out to be a long period of time.

Lack of Understanding

The reason most administrators don't understand high school journalism is that they haven't been involved with it in any real sense. No adviser has taken the time to explain the journalistic process to them, and they do not realize how important journalism is in the development of skills that are applicable to a variety of lifetime activities. It is possible you can make them aware of these facts.

To help prevent the administrators from ignoring journalism in the school, provide them with information about the program. Before the start of the school year, discuss with the school principal your plans and goals for the journalism students, and provide written documentation that can be studied and reviewed. Course syllabi, supply and equipment needs, staff organization rosters, and publication schedules are logical items to share with the principal.

Frequently, principals have the most difficulty understanding supply and equipment needs, so these should be especially well documented. For example, most principals will not readily allow a journalism program to have its own telephone; however, when a request for a telephone is accompanied by a complete explanation of why student journalists need unrestricted access to a telephone that allows direct-dial local calls, principals are less likely to refuse such a request without first giving it serious thought.

It also is important to provide the principal with descriptions of ideal student journalists, in terms of motivation, writing skills, and time availability. Make it clear to your supervisors that this journalism class should not be considered a dumping ground for students with learning problems or schedule conflicts.

Additionally, take your superiors on a pre-school tour of the journalism area, noting strengths and weaknesses. Periodic tours during the school year also are recommended, especially during times of high activity. This gives them an opportunity to see how complex the program really is. To support each tour, provide advance updates of what the staff members are working on, so your supervisor will have some context in which to place the information that is provided during the tour.

Also, ask the principal to place you on the agenda for faculty meetings at the school, for part of maintaining a high profile includes promoting the students' publications among colleagues. Faculty meetings also provide a platform to bring relevant publication matters to the attention of supervisors and colleagues.

A final suggestion for overcoming administrative lack of understanding is to discuss the finished publications with your superiors. Provide them with critiques of each edition of the student newspaper and yearbook. Make it standard procedure to request a meeting with them to obtain their reaction, and be sure to make the request before some element of their quirky displeasure prompts them to request a meeting to answer questions they may have.

Basically, to build understanding for the program, there needs to be a desire to establish a stream of constant communication with your supervisors by providing them with information and seeking their ideas. Such communication may be formalized, through writing, or it may be personalized, through face-to-face encounters. All communication, however, should contain a thread of continuity that makes the importance and needs of the journalism program more real to your audience.

Lack of Expectations

As you work to increase administrative understanding of the journalism program, there also should be an attempt to raise others' expectations for your program. In discussions with the principal, particularly when they concern uses of journalism and program goals you have in mind, describe the possibilities that the principal might otherwise never envision.

For example, to illustrate uses of journalism classes and student publications, describe them as integral parts of citizenship education. Be certain to point out the ways in which they support understanding of constitutional freedoms and serve as information exchanges in a democracy. Also, remind the principal that the publications support school spirit through their reporting on school activities, and that they serve both as historical records of the school and as public relations instruments.

While you might illustrate program goals through mere description, don't miss the chance to show your supervisor extreme examples of school publications, from nearby schools with enrollments similar to that at your school. These publications should illustrate the absolute worst and best in journalism, but the point should be that it is possible to do more with the program than has been done. To make this point, attempt to obtain publications from schools outside the local area, but this effort will only be rewarded if the publications teach your supervisor that the school's journalism can be better.

Additionally, when you provide your supervisors with critiques of students' work, they will see how strongly you believe that quality can improve. In fact, because of your critiques they may learn how to judge student publications and thereby become more interested in improving them.

The process to improve administrative expectations is similar to the process to improve administrative understanding, in that it is a continuous one which relies upon constant communication. You will find roadblocks to these efforts, but they are not insurmountable.

Lack of Support

Ultimately, support for the journalism program depends upon the degree to which administrators are motivated to improve the program. Their motivation is linked to their understanding of and expectations for the program, which in turn depends upon how convincing you are when explaining the various aspects of the program. This is why it is particularly important to present forceful arguments for the role of journalism in secondary education, the goals that have been set for this program, and the requirements the program needs.

When first meeting with your superiors to discuss the coming school year, have a well organized and prepared presentation During the school year, when preparing documentation and updates concerning the program, be sensitive to the environment and adapt these presentations to the characteristics of that environment. Some environments require advisers to be aggressive; others require forcefulness tempered with delicacy.

As well as providing information to administrators, there is a need to ask them for their ideas about the school's publications. Support can be gained by asking them to critique each publication, even if this means asking for only a general reaction, or by suggesting that they contribute a brief column of their own for each edition of the newspaper and a letter to students for each issue of the yearbook. Making them a part of the process often motivates the administrators to provide more support for publications.

Overall, a lot of time will be spent planting the seeds of ideas in administrators' minds. Seldom will immediate success for your ideas be achieved, but after a prolonged period, in which you nurture these ideas by repeating a prepared monologue on a monthly basis, some results may be seen. In the meantime, enthusiasm will have to be maintained and resources that are on hand will have to suffice. Eventually, you will gain some control over the situation, and the longer you stay at a given school, the easier it will be to achieve support for the journalism program.

Perhaps the most difficult task in overcoming the lack of administrative understanding, expectations, and support will be to overcome a lack of access to your superiors. There is no reason to expect that administrators will want to see you or that they would have time to see you as often as you would like. Surprisingly, they will not return telephone calls or respond to messages, and they will cancel appointments you make with them.

Do not despair. Keep sending them written material, and keep copies of what has been sent to them. Keep sending invitations to them to visit the journalism classroom, and continue asking them for ideas. Sooner or later, this persistence will be rewarded. Remember that you can be aggressive without being abrasive, and that when their collective ear is gained, you will have the opportunity to make great strides. Also, remember that you are not alone in this type of struggle, as other journalism teachers are fighting identical battles throughout the country.

CHAPTER 20

Beating the Budget Blues

When school administrators neither support student publications nor expect much from them, there is a good chance that funding for such publications is minimal. Thus efforts to change administrative attitudes toward the student newspaper and yearbook must be coupled with some independent steps to make the publications budget stretch as far as possible.

Naturally, if the principal is the main obstacle to increases in funding, and if you are relatively new to the school system, there may be some hesitancy to make immediate contact with higher authorities (the superintendent or the school board) in search of more revenue. You should, however, keep these possibilities in mind, as the principal may be reacting to a false perception of what others might support or tolerate.

After familiarizing yourself with the politics of the current environment, discuss this problematic plight with the principal. If you receive little or no satisfaction, aggressively but politely suggest that you and the principal take these arguments to the superintendent and the school board. Be prepared for the principal to reject this idea, but be persistent and pleasant. With enough prodding over a long period of time, eventually the principal will allow you to discuss these needs with those who make policy and create budgets.

When the opportunity is gained to confront the superintendent or the school board, use the same arguments made to convince the students (and perhaps your principal) that journalism is an important aspect of secondary education, and that student publications are very important historical records and public relations tools. At the very least, this well-organized presentation should include a brief comparison of publications among schools in the region and an analysis of various production costs over the past five years. Use the comparison to show what can be done with a proper budget, and be sure to include in this comparison superior publications from other schools similar in size and enrollment. The cost analysis should clearly show the price inflation that you and previous advisers have contended with in recent years.

Until administrative support for a bigger budget is obtained, continue to take advantage of other techniques that can either increase publication funding or help stretch the budget. These include methods of increasing revenues and diminishing expenses.

Increasing Your Revenues

In addition to the suggestions provided in Chapter 1, which dealt in part with increasing student motivation and enthusiasm concerning fund raising, and those in Chapter 14, which dealt in part with overcoming a deficit left by predecessors, there are a few other steps that can be taken to increase revenues for student publications.

One obvious avenue is to increase the advertising sales. Instead of adhering to the traditional format of display advertising, develop systems for classified advertisements and page sponsorship. For example, with student newspapers that are issued fairly frequently, the possibility for a booming classified advertising business always exists. If classified advertising is inexpensive enough and promoted well enough, it can bring in enough revenue to eliminate the need to charge readers for the publication. In turn, this will increase the publication's audience, which will justify an increase in charges for display advertising.

Another technique is to offer readers the opportunity to purchase inexpensive personal advertisements, but be very careful to draw up and publicize guidelines for such advertising. Some young people have a tendency to place personal advertisements that adults would judge to be in bad taste, if not worse. In their cleverness, some students also will create seemingly innocent advertisements that will have more than one meaning for their peers. Reserve the right to refuse questionable personal or classified advertising.

Page sponsorship, on the other hand, works well for yearbooks. Under this system, individuals (usually parents or businesses) are given lines of credit on yearbook pages that they "sponsor". Charges for sponsoring a page may vary, depending on the size and economic considerations of the area in which your school exists, but generally, $5-to-$10 per page is reasonable. Instruct the staff members to explain to potential buyers that for this fee, they will be named in a credit line at the bottom of the page or pages they agree to sponsor. The credit line might read, "This page is sponsored by John and Mary Doe".

Of course, more than one person may sponsor a page, as the parents of students who appear on sports and activity pages may wish to have their names associated with their children's pictures. This is fine, but be certain to make it clear to each sponsor that, for example, up to five individuals may sponsor any given page. Also, an option for exclusive sponsorship might be offered at a reduced price, e.g., $5/person/page for up to five people, or $20/page for an individual sponsor.

Another way to increase revenues is to sell pictures that the publication staff has taken. Pictures that have appeared in print are always in demand, and often there is a market for many of the pictures which were taken but not used. While the students might tend to wait until the end of the school year for such a sale, advise them that periodic picture sales can add enough money to the budget to allow for pizza parties and other rewards during the school year.

If you combine picture-selling with the suggestion in Chapter 1 to conduct special money-making activities, periodically hold special photography sessions in which

50

students are offered the opportunity to have candid pictures of themselves taken by the photography staff, for minimal charges. Prime times to hold such sessions are periods just prior to holidays requiring sweetheart gifts. Before implementing such a program, inquire about school policy concerning school fund-raising activities that compete with local businesses. It's possible that complaints from local photography studios could be directed at the publication for this practice.

One other way to increase revenues is to arrange a publications workshop at the school and charge other schools a registration fee to attend it. Invite media professionals and university professors to come to the school on a Saturday and lead workshops on writing, editing, photography, and design. This idea works well in regions containing a high concentration of schools with publications, but on a smaller scale, it also could work in areas with just a few schools whose students could benefit. To some extent, the success of such a project will depend upon the potential audience in the area and the economic health of the locale being served.

Diminishing Your Expenses

In the sense that it is used in this chapter, diminishing publication expenses means finding someone else to pay for the needs of the publications program. In Chapter 14, cutting corners were discussed as a means of reducing a deficit, and the ideas presented there can also be used to diminish expenses. It is, however, usually preferable to use someone else's money for certain expenses so large portions of the budget do not have to be spent for items that others will help to purchase.

In some school systems, student publications are expected to be self-sufficient. In others, either some formula to divide costs between the publications and the administration has been derived, or the administration has agreed to pay all costs, within prescribed limits. Whatever budgetary arrangement exists between the administration and student publications in the school, look for ways to decrease the amount of funds that must be used to maintain or improve the publication programs.

For example, if the administration is not contributing to the publication budgets, work to change that system. At the very least, work to convince the principal to help pay for high-cost items such as typewriters, computers, printers, copiers, camera equipment, light tables, and waxers. Also, attempt to work out an agreement stipulating that the administration will cover reasonable end-of-the-year deficits, defined according to expectations of costs and revenues.

If the administration contributes to the publication budgets according to some formula, work to shift the expense burden more toward the administration. This can be done based on inflation, depreciation and the wearing out of equipment, and changing economic projections for the local area. Do not be afraid to ask for more money, for if none is requested, the program will be ignored.

Another way to diminish expenses is to ask professionals and businesses in the local community to purchase new equipment for the journalism program or to underwrite the costs of such equipment. Presentations to the managers of local media outlets can be very effective, as can presentations to community groups such as the Chamber of Commerce and other civic organizations. Alumni of the school also can be major contributors of needed equipment.

When such people cannot be convinced to contribute money outright, try to convince them to donate used equipment to the program. Photography studios, for example, are always updating their camera equipment, and other businesses also buy new equipment every year. The program could be the beneficiary of this process, but it is necessary to let business leaders know that you have an interest in and a need for such equipment as cameras, furniture (desks, cabinets), typewriters, and computers. This idea can also be directed to the school system's administration and to the business skills program in the school. Both entities could be prime providers of used equipment.

In connection with overtures to school administrators and to the business skills program chairperson, be sure to obtain the names of those who service the business machines used in these areas. Service personnel can often give leads to inexpensive used or reconditioned equipment, and sometimes they will donate such equipment. If there is a salvage yard in the area, make it a point to visit it when equipment is needed. The already low prices that can be found there may be underwritten by someone in the community, especially if there is some publicity value in such a contribution. Make certain that potential contributors know that press releases concerning contributions to the journalism program will be mailed out to local media outlets.

Education cooperatives are other places to check when equipment is needed, for you may be able to share the cost of expensive items with other schools. For example, with the cooperative efforts of several advisers, typewriters or computers may be purchased through bulk orders, thereby reducing equipment costs. It's even possible that a typesetter no one school could afford to obtain by itself could be purchased by this cooperative type of group.

When it is impossible to purchase a typesetter, try to work out an agreement with a local publisher. The goal should be to allow the students to do their own typesetting, and some publishers will agree to let students come in after school or on weekends to do just that. The program might be more successful if it has a title such as "typesetting internship."

Concerning the costs of attending workshops, consider asking members of the community or local press organizations to sponsor trips for the journalism students, or inquire about money to underwrite the cost of having a workshop at the high school. As previously mentioned, other schools could be charged to attend workshops held at your school.

A final suggestion for reducing expenditures, while still obtaining what is needed, is to convince other departments to incorporate relevant costs into their budgets. For example, you may want the journalism students to have access to certain publications, but the budget may not contain enough revenue for subscriptions to such periodicals or allotments for such books. In this case, a discussion with the school librarian is appropriate. Ask that person to order the desired publications and have them paid for out of the library's budget. This idea can be applied equally well to other areas, such as the cost of supplies (call them instructional aids). Sometimes, success will depend upon the ingenuity used to label what is needed so that it falls within a category which can be covered by others.

Whether you work to increase revenues or diminish expenses, success depends upon how quickly you become an expert scavenger, manipulator, and debater. Often, success will require a good deal of work outside of school, and such work may take more time than you wish to spend. In the short run, when having little or no success, it may seem ridiculous to continue on this path. In the long run, it will definitely be worth the effort.

The longer you work in a school district, and the more familiar the system becomes, the easier it will be to work out a variety of funding compromises with the administration. The longer you live in a community, and the more highly visible you become, the easier it will be for the staff to obtain contributions from that community. Remember to keep long-term goals in mind, and let the small budgetary battles that are won sustain you as you fight the larger financial war.

CHAPTER 21
Maximizing Class Scheduling and Classroom Assignments

Few things can be as annoying to a journalism adviser as coping with class schedules and room assignments that undermine the smooth operation of a student publication. The problems associated with these inconveniences can be caused by lack of communication with administrators, insensitivity on the part of students, or lack of budget, but all such problems can be solved or at least significantly reduced in a relatively short time.

Class Scheduling

Three problems are associated with the scheduling of a journalism class that produces a publication. The first problem concerns the time of day the class is scheduled, the second problem involves the classes that compete with it, and the third problem has to do with not having a laboratory period in which the staff can work on the publication.

The time of day the class is scheduled is of primary importance because this can affect class enrollment and frequency of interruption. Specifically, the class should not be scheduled for afternoon class periods. Athletes who might want to be on staff also might have practice during the afternoon, and this conflict will greatly reduce their effectiveness as reporters, editors, photographers, or production staffers. Seniors, too, who potentially may be the best staff members, may want to leave school early (in school districts that permit this) so they may work or participate in other activities.

Additionally, classes scheduled in the afternoon are subject to a variety of interruptions, including but not limited to assemblies and other special activities, teacher conferences, and early closings for weather-related reasons. Such disruptions, which result in lost time, can be major reasons for production problems.

The major preventive measure that can be taken to avoid these problems is to discuss with the administration the importance of scheduling the journalism class in the morning. Simply explain how important it is for the publication to have access to athletes and seniors, and how important it is for the class not to have to lose time because of the interruptions noted above. Certainly, it should be early in the school year that the task of changing a bad schedule or keeping an existing good schedule should begin. Long before administrators start planning the next term's schedule, approach those in charge and plead your case. Keep track of the scheduling process and make frequent attempts to make these concerns known, at least until after receiving assurances that past efforts have been successful. Then write a note of thanks to those who were instrumental in changing the existing schedule.

While coping with a bad schedule, work on the athletes and seniors who have potential problems with their schedule. Talk with the athletes about taking journalism during the off-season, so they will be available when they are needed, and talk with the seniors about staying at school later than they normally would, to meet their obligations to the newspaper or yearbook. Explain the situation to counselors who approve students' schedules, and perhaps they will help you meet the goals desired. The biggest problem concerning student schedules is convincing the people involved that there is a problem.

In dealing with an inconveniet schedule, another step is to convince administrators not to interrupt afternoon classes with assemblies and other activities. At the very least, lobby for a more equitable day-long distribution of interruptions. For example, ask that at least half of the assemblies be held when the publication class does not meet. Other support can be gained for this idea from fellow teachers whose classes are consistent victims of such interruptions.

The second problem associated with class scheduling involves classes that compete with the journalism class. Problems arise particularly when class meets at the same time other required classes meet and when attractive new classes are scheduled for the same period. It is not reasonable to expect the journalism class to be "competition free" every term, but it is reasonable to ask that it, along with other required classes, be placed on a rotation system that allows students the chance to choose it during the same term in which they must take required courses. This is very necessary in school systems that recognize journalism as an activity rather than as a required course in a language-skills group.

When and if you are provided with ample warning that an attractive new class will be offered at the school, be sure to voice the opinion that it will draw students away from the journalism class if it is scheduled at the same time your class meets. Naturally, other teachers will have the same complaint, but make this concern known to avoid losing the scheduling battle merely because you were silent.

There is, however, a major advantage journalism advisers have over other teachers who will complain about this problem: advisers are in control of a ready-made publicity mill for their programs. As long as students view journalism as the interesting, exciting, and important activity that it really is, they will continue to sign up for it. This image can be maintained through the publicity that is given to journalism, so remember to do all that is possible to make journalism a high-visibility activity in the school by using any techniques available in your capacity as a member of the faculty.

The third problem associated with scheduling has to

do with situations in which publications are produced by journalism classes that also include great amounts of academic material. This adds up to an overload for the teacher, both in terms of mental and physical energy.

To alleviate this problem, the most important step is to present a well-organized argument to the administration, pointing out the reasons why you and the staff need a separate laboratory period to produce a publication. The presentation should include support from media professionals and post-secondary journalism professors, as well as comparisons with the journalism programs of other schools in the region. Another part of this effort should be a continuation of the attempt to convince administrators of journalism's importance in training students to survive in all aspects of their lives.

Another way to convince school administrators that a production laboratory is needed is to involve them in the production process, either directly or indirectly, so they see just how much work it takes to produce a publication. Insist that they tour the classroom during peak activity times, and aggressively work for their commitment to write a column for each issue of the publication, especially if the publication is a frequently issued newspaper.

While continuing the battle for a laboratory period, the problem of lack of time can be dealt with by enlisting the aid of other teachers. Explain the problem to them and work out agreements that will allow journalism students to pursue publication activities in nonjournalism classes. If permission is gained from other teachers to allow your students to work on their publication projects after they have finished the work which is specific to whatever other class is involved (e.g., English, art, or business), then the staff members will have extra time to complete their journalism tasks. For example, students in English classes could write or edit copy, students in art classes could create page designs or artwork, and students in business classes could type copy or work on advertising and record keeping. Such activity might actually appeal to teachers involved in teaching tasks similar to the ones the staff members may be completing.

One final tactic to pursue, although its success rate is often low, is to encourage key staff members to schedule a study hall together, which could be used as an extra work period for publication-related activities. In this same vein, inquire as to whether staff members could work before or after school, or during lunch periods. It is amazing how much work can be done by organized students during very short breaks (15-20 minutes), and sometimes, it is just enough to allow you to do what needs to be done in journalism class.

Classroom Assignments

The problems associated with classroom assignments can be related to class scheduling problems, although they are significantly different. Primarily, the problems have to do with (1) your movement during the day and (2) space problems for the production staff.

For a variety of reasons, it is counter-productive for other teachers to hold classes in the production room. Teenagers often yield to their curiosity, and if given the opportunity, they will investigate whatever the journalism staff leaves within reach. This often causes annoying problems and sometimes results in missing material (especially pictures). It also means that staff members cannot leave ongoing projects in a condition which would allow a quick return to work. When students who are not associated with the publication populate the classroom without proper supervision, staff members will have to "lock up shop" to ensure that their work is secure, thus necessitating time to "set up shop" when they return. This "locking up" and "setting up" simply is a waste of valuable time. You need a classroom you can lock up when it's empty.

Additionally, if it is not possible to call a single classroom home, staff members will have difficulty finding you when they need advice and direction during the day. As the adviser, there is a necessity to be located in a central area so staff members may find you to ask questions and receive assignments without delay. Share these matters with school administrators and explain to them that it is a prime concern of yours.

To combat the problems that arise from unnecessary movement during the day, it may be essential to point out these needs and problems to the administration. While this mode of operation may not solve the problem completely during your first year in a school system, try to work on a compromise schedule that would allow you to stay in one room for large portions of the day. If the school has no designated journalism room, work to establish one by meeting with your superior and explaining its importance.

If the journalism room must be relinquished occasionally, it should contain cabinets and lockers that can be locked. Additionally, the room should be equipped with sufficient shelves, tables and chairs (for typewriters, computers, and layout and paste-up activities), and closets with doors that can be locked. This implies that the classroom should be large enough to comfortably conduct the production process.

If the room is not well equipped, do all that is possible to improve it. Talk with administrators, plead with community groups and businesses, and work out arrangements with industrial arts teachers to have their students build furniture and closets that are custom designed for the staff members' needs. Also, consider attending garage sales and flea markets or visiting second-hand shops and salvage yards to obtain inexpensive goods that meet classroom needs. At the very least, obtain separate containers that may be stacked, for staff members can use these easily accessible containers to store their materials. Locally placed advertisements that request donations of specified equipment sometimes are successful in adding to the journalism room's inventory.

If the room is too small, demonstrate this by insisting that administrators visit the classroom during production periods, to see for themselves how difficult it is for students to work under current circumstances. Explain how counter-productive it is to operate without adequate breathing room, as there is a continual need to shift materials or put them away in order to pursue other necessary tasks. This wastes time and interrupts the natural flow of production activity. After you have pursued this goal for several months without obtaining a positive administrative response, intensify the lobbying efforts so the needs of the staff members are not forgotten.

The problems associated with class scheduling and class assignments are not insurmountable, but while you work to overcome them, they may seem to make life impossible. Take whatever steps you can to alleviate as many small problems in these areas as possible, as this will make the larger ones seem more tolerable. Then, during the school year, create a list of larger goals to pursue, and do what you can to reach those goals. Celebrate when you reach one, and don't let defeat get you down. There's always next year.

CHAPTER 22

Looking Forward to Bidding the Publication

If the publication program involves the use of outside photography, typesetting, paste-up, or printing, try to obtain the most service for the least amount of money. Advisers who are new to a school system or who work in a system in which administrators handle all contracts may find it difficult to become a part of the process, but it is important that they develop their influence in this area. Essentially, problems arise when administrators ignore the need for suggestions from advisers, when contracts are not re-bid every year, and when contracts are incomplete.

Administrative Authoritarianism

In school systems located in small towns or other sparsely populated areas, it may be difficult to find more than one local photography studio, typesetting company, or printing establishment that can handle the publication's photographic or production needs. Thus to meet those needs, you may be forced to rely upon friends or relatives of your administrative superiors. The friend or relative may not be of a preferred choice, and it may be made clear that this situation cannot be changed.

This could be unfortunate, both in terms of service and cost, but often there is little that can be done about it in any immediate sense. It is possible, however, to make a long-term effort to improve the situation by making up your own bidsheets and conducting research to locate other businesses capable of servicing the publication needs. If contractors cannot be changed, at least try to create contracts that are more favorable for the operation.

Most of your effort may be spent trying to gain acceptance as a contributor to the bidding process. To convince superiors that you should play an active role in this activity, remind them that you have a more complete knowledge of the situation than they do, and that you are more familiar with the demands contractors must meet to make the publication program an optimal success. Also, remind them that the program's success depends in part upon how competitive the bidding process is and upon how complete the contracts are. Through your suggestions, both areas can be improved.

Obtaining Bids

The first step in the process of obtaining bids is to find out the names of companies that provide the types of services needed by the staff. To do this, contact high school advisers in the area and ask them which companies they use and how they would rate these companies. Other information that may be useful can be obtained from journalism advisers in the colleges and universities in the area.

Portrait studios throughout the country send out teams of photographers in the fall to take yearbook portraits, so don't feel that by nature of location a local portrait studio must be used. If you have a good relationship with such a studio, in terms of special photographic work that is done for the yearbook or newspaper at special rates or in terms of training the staff photographers, consider retaining the company as the publications portrait photographer, even if its rates are higher than those of more distant companies. Not only would that be good for the established relationship, but it is more convenient at times when retakes are necessary.

Likewise, local typesetters are preferred to ones located in distant areas, as it is possible to make overnight changes with little trouble when the typesetting machine is within easy driving distance.

In situations involving outside printers, quality often does not depend upon whether the printer is near or far, although it is good to be able to judge color signatures (the pages with color pictures) as they come off the presses, just in case there are adjustments to be made. Distance, however, could make a big difference in shipping prices, as interstate trucking and rail rates are based on a combination of weight and distance. If a distant printer is used, be certain to obtain written estimates of shipping charges.

Regardless of how many companies you locate for various production needs, send bidsheets to all of them every year, and let it be known this process will be conducted annually. Such publicity serves as a reminder to current contractors that they cannot become complacent in their dealings with the student publication, and sometimes it can lead to a two- or three-year contract that limits inflationary jumps in prices.

Creating A Complete Contract

If a contract form is provided by the company doing the bidding, you may be at a big disadvantage because such contracts often favor the contractors. To avoid this dilemma, make up your own bid sheets after talking with publication advisers in the area and obtaining blank bid sheets from companies likely to serve your needs.

Concerning photography bids for yearbook portraits, be certain to have in writing the financial arrangements that have been agreed upon by both parties and the deadlines for receiving proofs. If the school enrollment is large, it would be normal to expect a large number of students to order additional prints from the photographer; in this case, ask for a rebate based on either of two variables: the number of students having their pictures taken or the number ordering prints from the photographer. It is not unreasonable to ask for 25 cents for each student who is photographed or 50 cents for each student who orders prints, and the option to use whichever formula yields more of a rebate.

Another item to include involves photographic materials. Note that the studio should provide the staff with film and film processing materials at cost. If staff members process their own film, this arrangement results in generous savings.

A guarantee should also be sought from the studio that it will provide the photography staff with appropriate publicity and administrative forms to use before the portrait session dates, that the studio will provide its own secretarial help during the session dates, and that the studio will prepare the yearbook portraits for the printer, according to printer specifications.

Where typesetting and paste-up bids are concerned, obtaining specific prices for the types of work that will need to be done is imperative. For example, obtain rates for the following items: typesetting body copy, headlines, photocaptions, and charts; error correction (you should have to pay for author corrections only); graphic arts and special effects; and page paste-up, if the staff members are not going to do it.

"Turnaround" schedules also need to be obtained in writing. Make sure they are realistic and that they will accommodate your needs. These schedules designate the amount of time you are willing to allow for specific types of work to be done. It is not unreasonable to ask for a two-day turnaround time for typesetting by local companies, while a longer time may be required for distant companies. Paste-up turnaround time will vary according to several factors, but a schedule that exceeds five working days for local companies should be considered excessive. Distant companies should be willing to pay delivery charges for completed work, so be certain the contract addresses this issue.

When creating a contract or bid sheet for a printer, include the standard items. For yearbook bid sheets, indicate the number of books, number of pages, trim size of pages (usually 9 X 12, 8½ X 11, or 7¾ X 10½), calendar date for last day to adjust number of books or pages, quality and weight of paper (80-pound stock is normal), method of binding (Smythe sewn is most common), cover specifications, cost of four-color and spot color, and terms of payment (usually designated as three separate payments spaced throughout the year, the last of which is due after the books are delivered).

Some special items that should be included in a yearbook bid sheet are cost of proofs; sales tax rate (the school's tax identification number may eliminate sales taxes in some states); delivery charges (which are often overlooked by new advisers); charges for correcting author errors; costs for screens, graphic lines (sometimes called tool lines), and other graphic arts work; costs for photographs and special photographic effects such as duotones or posterization; and charges/credits for more/fewer copies, pages, four-color signatures, and spot color signatures. You also might add a category designating the minimum number of visits a printer's representative will make to the school and the minimum number of workshops that a representative will hold for the staff during such visits. Additionally, there should be some statement about compensation for deadlines missed by the staff (in submitting their completed pages) and by the printer (in delivering proof sheets and final product).

If you advise a newspaper, the yearbook bid sheet can be adapted to your needs after making a list of all the services that will be required from a printer. If the newspaper printer is nearby, you might be able to arrange special services for photographic processing as a part of the bid, so be sure to inquire about those possibilities before you create the bid sheet.

Overall, bidding the publication can be an exciting process if the administrators allow you to take part in it. You will be amazed at the amounts of money that can be saved and how much service can obtained for the effort. The key, of course, is to create a thorough bid sheet that is used mercilessly every year, and with a minimal amount of research, a treasure-chest of help for yourself and your staff can be unlocked and utilized.

CHAPTER 23

Meeting Censorship Wisely

Battles over control of publication content are potentially the most explosive types of conflict in which you and your staff members may become involved. As an adviser, it may not matter to you if school administrators support the coverage of controversial issues in the student newspaper or yearbook. This may be especially true if you believe that allowing the staff members to write editorials and stories about issues of concern to the school community will result in termination of your employment.

On the other hand, however, administrative censorship may be of some concern, but you may not know how to combat it. This might be particularly annoying when the journalism students discuss freedom of the press, and there has to be an admission to them that although they have this constitutional right as citizens, they cannot exercise it fully at school as students, in their publications.

The most desirable ways to resolve a censorship conflict concerning student publications do not involve legal action. Instead, they involve efforts to promote understanding among administrators and students, and efforts to promote compromise between administrators and students.

Promote Understanding

In order to promote understanding about the First Amendment rights that student publications enjoy, familiarize yourself with legal decisions that apply to the state. While the U.S. Supreme Court decisions in the areas of free speech and press apply to all states, decisions of other federal courts and decisions of state courts have limited jurisdictions. Notably, the U.S. Supreme Court has upheld administrative censorship of high school publications produced as laboratory exercises of journalism classes. Several publications explaining the Court's position are listed in Section V of this handbook.

If you are unfamiliar with state or regional court rulings on high school publications, consult with local university professors who teach media law. They should be able to provide an overview of the legal holdings that apply to advisers, the principal as administrative censor, and students as reporters and editors. Be advised, however, that regardless of the law, administrators sometimes exceed their legal boundaries. Also be advised that just because an administrator has the right to censor student speech, it doesn't automatically follow that the administrator must exercise that right.

Once you know the boundaries of the law in your state, it is important to find out what the school administrators know about such boundaries and if they care about them. At the earliest possible time, preferably before the start of the school year, arrange to meet with the principal to discuss student press rights. This should not be a hostile meeting, but assume that the school administrator's view of student publications and censorship will be more conservative than yours. The goal of this meeting should be to obtain a clear understanding of the principal's position and to provide the principal with a clear understanding of your knowledge of the law. Then, if the two of you are very far apart in your positions concerning what may appear in student publications, the real negotiations can begin. These negotiations probably will be continuous, over a period of years.

Merely discussing the First Amendment rights of students with the administrators, in spite of the fact that they may not enjoy the discussion, makes them aware of your beliefs and knowledge. In a subtle way, this is important, for it is a signal to them that they are not dealing with an ignorant person.

During the course of these discussions, make sure to allude to the fact that journalism coursework will include the First Amendment, which they also will be learning about in the portions of their history and social studies classes that focus on the U.S. Constitution. The goal here is to point out how disconcerting it will be for you to teach a principle that cannot be practiced to its reasonable limits.

This discussion will lead to another point, which concerns the reasonable limits to students' free press rights. Although advisers are legally considered an "arm of the state" if they are teaching at a public school, and although they are subject to a censorship suit if there is unreasonable interference with the content of a student publication, assure the school administrators that you have no intention of encouraging the students to publish irresponsible material. In fact, it would be very helpful to assure them that you will teach responsible journalism in the journalism classes and do all that is humanly possible to keep obscene, libelous, and other harmful or disruptive information out of print.

You should, however, argue that in the high school environment there will be occasions when controversial items of public concern will need to be discussed in print. Guarantee the principal that coverage will be balanced. Think about offering the opportunity for administrative participation that could come in the form of a letter to students and which should appear in the editorial section of whatever publication is involved. Such a suggestion often opens the door to a previously closed administrative mind.

If necessary, to promote understanding among all authority figures who might have concerns about the content of student publications, also arrange to meet with school board members and PTA members. The more support that can be mustered for openness, the more success you will have in advising a meaningful publication and avoiding censorship conflict.

The staff members comprise the other group of people to whom you must explain your position, for they, too, will interpret the First Amendment differently from the courts. In teaching them about press freedom, make it a point to stress that with press freedom comes responsibility, and that because they practice journalism in a special environment, their freedom is somewhat less than that enjoyed by professional journalists. This does not mean they can publish only bland material, but it does mean they must consider more variables than their professional counterparts.

It is your job to teach students that these variables generally concern aspects of audience maturity. When they understand that because of age and lack of worldly experience, some readers are not equipped emotionally to cope with some material (controversial or otherwise), they will also understand why courts have said it would not be in the best interests of the school to publish certain types of stories. While advisers may not agree with such court decisions, it is not their right to ignore them.

When all possible steps have been taken to promote administrative and student understanding of press freedom in public secondary schools, the next step will be to promote compromise between administrators and students.

Promote Compromise

Although administrators may strictly censor student publications in the school, it is desirable to avoid that alternative. To keep administrators and student journalists from harboring ill feelings toward each other due to differences of opinion over student press rights, attempt to lead them to a mutually agreed upon compromise in this area. This can be accomplished by several techniques.

As you discuss with the administrators your views on student press rights, try to determine where they are vulnerable, in terms of the issues on which they might bend their position. By providing them with a list of potential controversial story ideas, you might obtain permission to pursue at least some stories that will make readers sit up and take notice. Don't expect to receive their blessings for stories involving or alluding to teenagers' sexual activity, school board politics, or teacher evaluations, but by including these topics on the list, other controversial items become less controversial in comparison. Thus permission may be obtained for the students to write about divorce, suicide, and drugs.

Another technique to use with administrators is to show them the types of articles that have appeared in other high school publications. While it may take some time to collect such information, if you join a high school press association or a journalism education association, you will soon have access to a variety of relevant material.

Alerting administrators to the censorship battles that high school administrators have lost in court may also be useful to this non-censorship campaign. Information of this nature may be obtained from media law texts, education journals, and media law professors. If the decision is made to pursue this tactic, use as much diplomacy as possible.

At the same time you are attempting to move your superiors toward compromise, it may be necessary and useful to move the students toward compromise as well.

The students may be easier targets, but remember to treat them with respect to maintain their respect.

Unless you are prepared to encourage the students to sue the school administration over a censorship issue (and, perhaps, engage in litigation to obtain a teaching contract for subsequent years), there is a need to convince staff members that they must, for the moment, accept less freedom to publish than they are entitled to as citizens. While this is a grim situation, at least from the standpoint of student press rights, it is a compromise that economic reality forces most advisers to accept; most advisers do not wish to jeopardize their jobs. Of course, advisers are ostensibly terminated for reasons other than for expressing their opinions, but unless you are willing and able to pursue a court battle to claim otherwise, learn to live within the system until there is a chance to change it.

To convince the students that compromise is appropriate, explain to them that change takes a long time, and that you will continue to work for it even after they have graduated. This provides the students with a long-term view that may help to ease their outrage.

In discussions with the staff, also note that compromise neither prevents them from publishing all important information nor diminishes their role as a conduit for expression in the school community. Convince them that to continue publication is their most important goal, and if temporary compromise is required, the sacrifice is worthwhile.

As noted above, students frequently will be more agreeable to compromise than will administrators, for students are used to being subservient to authority. This does not mean that they should not be taught about their rights, but it does mean that you enjoy more of an advantage with them than with school administrators. However this situation is handled, be honest with the students.

One other technique that might be employed to promote compromise is to arrange meetings between students and administrators, in which they can discuss the problem and their philosophies concerning it. Such meetings provide opportunities to bring ideas into the open, and if the staff members are coached in advance not to become emotional over the outrageous philosophical positions the principal and school board members hold, there exists the potential to discover common ground. Such discoveries are your goals.

Although administrative censorship may be difficult to endure, it is not necessarily either permanent or complete. In fact, your state may adopt a student press law that virtually neutralizes U.S. Supreme Court decisions supporting administrative censorship. Five states have done so already. Regardless of the legal situation, as an adviser, you may be caught between administrative incompetence and student desire, and you must forge a path between the two. While it may be an undesirable task, it is one worthy of vigorous pursuit.

CHAPTER 24

Resolving Requests for Favors

Because many high school administrators do not understand journalism's editorial, production, and distribution processes, they do not hesitate to make journalistically awkward requests of advisers. Although some requests are reasonable (and it certainly is good public relations for you to honor them), when a request interferes with the editorial process associated with student publications or creates extra work for you and the staff, explain the problem to the person making the request.

Editorial Interference

For the purposes of this discussion, editorial interference does not mean censorship, although some scholars have defined any editorial requests by administrators as censorship. Instead, as used here, editorial interference refers to outrageous administrative requests to insert information into the publication. Frequently, principals and others will ask that a student publication include notices of meetings or events related to the school environment, and such requests are reasonable. In contrast, some requests should be resisted.

For example, administrators often desire to see certain types of stories in print. Sometimes they will ask that the student editors play the role of "cheerleader" for the school, by suggesting they run either stories or editorials that support administrative goals. Such requests are likely to be made during campaigns for community votes concerning school funding or in times when controversies engulf the school system.

When the publication has received such a request, advise the person who makes it that the editors will discuss it, but explain that you cannot guarantee the staff members' willingness to comply. Once again, define the importance of editorial discretion, and make it clear that the editors judge all editorial ideas on the basis of merit. Of course, it is your responsibility to discuss with the editors the positive and negative aspects of each story idea received from your superiors.

Occasionally, the administration will want to see supportive stories in the student press. Because of this, it is a good reason to hold pre-school meetings with the principal and school superintendent, to discuss the journalistic guidelines the staff will be following. If administrators know in advance, through your tactful presentation, that they cannot expect student publications to be 100 percent supportive of administrative policy and desires, some undesirable requests for editorial favors may never be made. This does not mean that all requests to create or "tone down" editorial sentiment will cease, but the number of such requests should diminish.

Another type of request that interferes with the students' decisions about publication content flows from administrators' promises to their business associates. You may be asked to publish free advertising that promotes businesses owned or operated by friends of administrators, and there is justification for refusing such requests. The possibility of such requests is a good reason to develop and publish a pre-school advertising policy and rate schedule that is strictly followed.

Extra Work

The second area in which requests for favors are frequent is related primarily to distribution of student publications, although it occasionally includes editorial problems as well. Sometimes, administrators will ask to make exceptions to the yearbook distribution policy and make requests to give copies of the yearbook, to selected individuals, prior to the planned distribution date.

This may not cause extra paperwork, but if the yearbooks have been customized in some way (e.g., student names stamped on the covers), it may take an inordinate amount of time to search the shipment for the requested books. Attempt to explain this problem to the person making the request, and ask that person to search for the desired yearbook in the event that you cannot find the time to do so. Seldom should the time be found to complete this request.

Other favors that require extra work for the staff involve requests for certain types of editorial content (as mentioned earlier in this chapter), but some of the problems they cause have to do with the timing of those requests. If the administrators have not yet been convinced that journalism is a serious undertaking that requires planning and adherence to deadlines, they will ignore the pre-publication deadline schedules and expect you and the staff to comply with their requests, regardless of the timing.

Even when the requested editorial content is acceptable to the staff members for inclusion in the publication, the poor timing of such requests may create extra work. It could mean changing page designs and redoing pages that already have been pasted up. This is very time consuming and should be avoided whenever possible. It is up to the adviser to resist administrative requests that will cause such problems.

As a general rule, to avoid being the target of requests for favors, fully explain the operating policies to those people who are likely to make such requests. Also, publish the guidelines under which the publication will operate, as such guidelines provide reference points from which to expand the defense against encroachments on reasonable publication-related procedures.

CHAPTER 25
Handling Personnel Changes

Administrators may be involved in three types of personnel changes that may cause problems for publications advisers. One type concerns changes within the administration, another concerns changes involving advisers, and the third concerns changes among the publication staff. Any of these changes, if not dealt with properly, can significantly affect the publication operation.

Changes Involving Administrators

When high school principals are replaced and when the make-up of the local school board is altered through appointment or election, student publications may benefit or suffer. The outcome depends upon your relationship with the outgoing administrators and upon the views of the incoming administrators.

If there has been success in building a pleasant relationship with the administrators, in that they have supported the program in most of the ways available to them, then valuable allies to the publication will be lost when they leave. On the other hand, if they have not been very cooperative in building a reasonably workable operation, seize the opportunity to convince their replacements that journalism is a valuable program with special needs.

When the outgoing administrators are allies, suggest that they discuss the journalism program and its special needs with their successors. Support such as this allows the relationship with new administrators to begin in a positive way. At the very first opportunity, make an appointment to talk with new administrators about the journalism program, so that from the start they will know your expectations of them. Schedule appointments with them and provide them with a comprehensive overview of the needs and goals of the newspaper and yearbook. Also, offer them the same information and opportunities for suggestions that were successfully shared with their predecessors.

If the outgoing administrators have not been cooperative allies with the program, view their departure as an opportunity to build meaningful relationships with their successors. Take the same steps that would be normally taken by teachers moving into a new position as journalism adviser.

The main point is that it's not wise to sit back and hope for the best when new administrators arrive on the scene. It is a must to take aggressive steps to ensure the success of the program, and that means laying the ground work for a supportive relationship with new superiors and maintaining a professional profile that is highly visible to them.

Changes Involving Advisers

As discussed in Chapter 14, certain problems may occur when you step into a position recently vacated by a well-liked adviser. While those problems have been adequately addressed in that chapter, there is another problem, related to changes in advisers, which needs some comment in the current context.

In the event that you are the adviser who is being replaced, either voluntarily or involuntarily, take it upon yourself to extend to your replacement all of the support that can be offered. Explain to the staff the reasons for departing, urge them to give their full support to the new adviser, and introduce the new adviser to the staff if circumstances allow such a meeting.

Additionally, offer to meet with the new adviser to provide a complete overview of the journalism program, including but not limited to its strengths and weaknesses, its relationship with the administration, and its most promising students. If you decide to depart in the middle of a school year, leave your replacement with enough information about ongoing projects so important deadlines will be met and so nothing the staff has started will go unfinished. Unless someone takes the time to tell them about the quirks in the operation, new advisers will be victimized by the same pitfalls you encountered in your tenure as adviser.

Remember, even if the departure is involuntary, try not to be inhumane to the innocent person who is the replacement. After all, it is your former students and their high school journalism that will suffer the most from a change involving an uninitiated replacement.

Changes Involving Students

This topic, like changes involving advisers, also has been discussed in an earlier chapter, but the current discussion focuses on student staff changes caused by administrators, rather than on changes brought about by students or by other circumstances. The discussion also focuses on preventing the changes rather than on coping with them.

For example, administrators may endorse a policy of placing unqualified students in journalism classes that produce publications. They may not do this intentionally, as they may not understand the intricacies of journalism, but whether they mean to do so or not, it is the adviser who will suffer when this policy is allowed to continue. When such personnel are introduced into what has been built into a workable operation, the operation may break down.

To protect the staff from having to deal with the disruption caused by unqualified students, explain to your administrators that journalism should not be viewed as a dumping ground for problem students. In the sense it is used here, the term "administrators" refers to those people who decide which students are placed in your classes. Frequently, the school's guidance counselors will be the major forces in determining class make-up, so talk with each counselor before student class schedules are created. It might be a good practice to touch base with guidance counselors each term, both as a reminder about unqualified students and as a recruitment device for talented ones.

Although you may feel that you have little control over the personnel changes described in this chapter, your influence, before or after they take place, can be felt more frequently than what might be expected. If you are aware of the possibilities associated with appropriately timed action, you can make a big difference.

SECTION IV
SOLVING OTHER PROBLEMS

CHAPTER 26

Clarifying Adviser/Journalist Roles

In general, people do not understand the role of publication adviser, and they do not understand the specific roles of student journalists. Because the term "people" refers to administrators, teachers, students, parents, and other members of the community, the publication staff may receive a lot of criticism for not meeting the expectations these people have. Your awareness of these expectations can prevent the misunderstandings they can cause.

False Expectations

Although the adviser is not the editor of a student publication, the people who know you in your capacity as adviser often will think you have complete control over the publication. This means blame will be placed on your shoulders both for items that appear in print and for items that are excluded.

Concerning items that do appear in print, criticism may result for a number of reasons. Some people will want the staff to publish only the information that has been provided, and thus when staff members print additional information, such as more than one side of any given story, or write editorial commentary about the subject, sources become angry.

Additionally, because they do not understand the editing process, sources will be unhappy with the ways stories are written, the choices of quotations, and the pictures that are used. Their complaints will be that the stories do not emphasize the most important items; that the quotations are irrelevant, wrong, or used out of context; and that the pictures do not show all they should show.

Some of the complaints will be well-founded simply because the editorial process does occasionally break down. That is to be expected of a high school journalism staff, although the number of times this occurs should diminish greatly during the course of the school year. Still, many complaints will occur because people do not know how journalists choose material for publication. For example, they do not realize the extent to which time and space constraints dictate which material appears in print and how that material looks.

People also will expect professionalism and maturity from students who are neither professional nor mature. Despite your guidance, some headlines will be misleading; stories will contain misspellings, grammatical errors, and factual errors; important aspects of a story will be ignored; people will be misquoted; photographs will be out of focus or poorly framed; and picture captions will be incomplete or inaccurate. To make matters worse, the immaturity of some staff members will result in the publication of material that most adults would consider silly, inappropriate, or distasteful.

While you will do your best to instill in your staff members the characteristics of professional journalists, you will not (and you should not) control everything that appears in print. Through the processes of teaching and consultation, you will give valuable direction to the publication, and eventually it will improve; however, while awaiting these improvements in the publication, there is a need to take preventive measures to limit the false expectations others will have about it.

Preventive Measures

One way to help protect yourself and your staff members from criticism resulting from false expectations is to replace those expectations with realistic ones. In a multi-faceted, ongoing educational process, you and your staff can teach would-be critics enough about the journalistic process to reduce the amount of criticism they generate.

For example, if you create, publish, and distribute guidelines concerning editorial contributions to student publications, you can refer to them when dealing with people who ask the staff to include only certain information in the publications. Thus if you specify in the guidelines that not all material contributed for publication will be published, that material which is accepted is subject to editing, and that publication also depends somewhat upon deadline requirements and space availability, you will avert many problems.

Similarly, if the guidelines specify the form in which written copy or photographs should be presented (and the deadlines for accepting such material), contributors can be alerted to the fact that the staff will not blindly accept all material, in any form, at any time. Once these guidelines become common knowledge, which may take some time, those who wish to have material published will be more conscientious about preparing and delivering it to your staff.

To increase the effectiveness of editorial guidelines, especially when they are distributed to people who will be repeat contributors to the publication, e.g., representatives from student government, secretaries of school clubs, and coaches of the school's competitive teams, they should be accompanied by standardized forms that designate the type of information your staff desires. These forms generally follow a fill-in-the-blank format that prompts the person filling them out to provide basic information (names, dates, places, significance of events) that otherwise might be overlooked by untrained observers.

Another preventive measure that might raise the journalistic consciousness of repeat contributors is to hold an informational workshop for them at the beginning of the school year. Consider designating these people as correspondents who would be responsible for reporting newsworthy events to student publications. If they can be trained to respect deadlines and complete the standardized forms described above, then on a regular

66

basis the staff will receive publishable information that won't need too much adjustment.

Through training, the correspondents will learn what is expected of them, and they will learn what to expect from student publications if deadlines are not met or if material is incomplete. Creating such a relationship with various people in the school system will diminish the amount of criticism you and your staff will receive.

At the beginning of the school year, you also might create and distribute a survey designed to measure reader interest in the types of material that have appeared in student publications over the preceding two years. This not only provides readers with a reminder of what to expect, but it allows the staff the opportunity to find out what is well liked in a publication and what does not appeal to the audience. While student publications cannot please everyone, the adoption of some suggestions obtained through surveys often can improve a publication's appeal.

Finally, an ongoing step that staff members can take to reduce false expectations is to conduct a continuous public relations program for their publications. As indicated in earlier chapters, such a program can be used for a variety of purposes, and one of them could be to make publication procedures and requirements highly visible to the people most likely to overlook them.

This means that you publicize deadlines in the appropriate circulars teachers and administrators receive, that deadlines are posted outside of the journalism room, and that the editors publish deadlines in each issue of the newspaper. It also means that someone from the publication staff should be designated to remind club and organizational secretaries of deadlines, and that whenever you attend staff meetings, it is your responsibility to mention upcoming deadlines.

A public relations program also may be used to educate people about the ways copy and photographs are prepared and chosen for publication. Through personal visits to clubs and organizations, you and the staff can eliminate many potential problems.

Short presentations to such groups can alert the members to the needs of student publications and to the time and space problems they face. Remember, most people who have not been involved with student publications have no knowledge of the obstacles publication staffs encounter on a daily basis. Informing them of the problems gives them a more realistic perspective on which to base their expectations.

Whatever methods are employed to prevent the false expectations that people develop concerning student publications, you never will eliminate all of the problems that flow from such expectations. Don't worry. After a few years as an adviser, you will develop special preventive techniques to fit the circumstances peculiar to your environment. You also will develop a "thick skin" to help you cope with problems you cannot prevent.

CHAPTER 27

Encouraging Students Not Involved in Journalism

Regardless of your experience as a student publication adviser, you probably will never outgrow your astonishment at the lack of enthusiasm toward journalism that members of the student body will demonstrate. In fact, the journalistic apathy that you will encounter from some students not involved in journalism will make some of your unenthusiastic staff members seem like journalistic cheerleaders!

Part of the problem may be a general lack of school spirit, but a lack of understanding about student publications also can contribute to lack of interest in student newspapers and yearbooks. You and your staff can do a lot to change such attitudes.

Lack of School Spirit

If lack of school spirit is having a detrimental effect on the interest that student publications generate, you and the staff must use your positions to help change the situation. Generally, professional journalists avoid the role of community cheerleader, except perhaps in the areas of sports or civic improvement, and thus the staff needs to know that cheerleading in student publications must be limited. That does not mean, however, that the staff members' high visibility in the school community cannot be used to promote school spirit in other ways.

One way to promote school spirit, which later will translate into interest in student publications, is to sponsor and publicize events that will create interest in the school. For example, the journalism program could sponsor sports events involving competition between faculty and students, administrators and students, or faculty and administrators. Noncompetitive events such as dances, bonfires, and school beautification programs also promote school spirit.

Another way to promote positive attitudes toward the school is to publish positive material about school activities and members of the student body. This can be done without violating journalistic standards of objectivity, although staff members should be cautioned not to paint such a rosy picture of the school that their publications lose credibility.

The types of positive material that will increase interest in both the school and student publications include coverage of the winners of scholarships and awards, stories about school improvements that affect students (e.g., better services, better instruction, and better facilities), and items that include material generated by students. The latter category includes items such as student surveys involving topics of interest to the student body, student letters to the editor, and student comments about specified topics.

To encourage student involvement, the staff may want to create a suggestion box for student publications. Some suggestions may then be published in the newspaper, with an editor's note asking for additional student opinion. As the adviser, consider asking the school's English teachers if they would assign an essay concerning student publications and their content.

You might also propose that the journalism staff sponsor writing and photography contests for students not involved in journalism. Winners would have their work published in either the newspaper or yearbook, depending on the specific situation. Topics for the contests could reflect something positive about the school.

All of the above-mentioned ideas lead to increased student interest in student publications because they all promote either involvement in school activities or better perceptions of the school environment. When students become involved and perceive their school as a positive place to be, their school spirit almost always improves. In turn, their desire to read about their school and the people in it also will improve, and student publications will benefit from this change.

Promoting Student Publications

In addition to directly or indirectly promoting school spirit, a lot can be done by the staff to directly promote student publications. This may begin with guaranteeing that the students are enthusiastic about the publications they work on, and that they share this enthusiasm with their friends who are not staff members.

The campaign also should have as one of its aims the promotion of student publications as important aspects of the school environment. While you will have touched upon this in your public relations contacts with administrators and other teachers, staff members need to develop and share this attitude with their peers.

Only when an audience views a media outlet as valuable will it take an interest in that outlet. Thus it is important to develop in audience members the idea that student publications not only serve their interests, but need their contributions and support. This philosophy can be promoted in editorials and used with the suggestions for student involvement noted earlier in this chapter.

Other ways to help increase the perceived value of student publications include increasing the quality of their content, winning publication contests, and discussing their value as historical records.

To increase the quality of publication content, the staff must be sensitive to audience needs and take extraordinary care in copy preparation. This means expanding the categories for types of stories covered, researching topics so that in-depth stories are published, and covering people who would not normally find their names in print. If the publication includes pictures, more than normal care should be taken in all aspects of photography.

Increasing the publication's content quality will

attract more readers, and the publication will more likely win awards when it is entered in contests. This is important because award-winning publications generate staff spirit as well as student interest. As you can see, creating pride of this nature can help advisers in several ways. Of course, the staff should publicize in their newspaper and in the community newspaper the fact that student publications have won awards.

One other way to promote interest in student publications is to explain to the potential audience that such publications serve as historical records for an important portion of their lives. Twenty years from the time students complete high school, their memories will have faded somewhat, and looking through old newspapers and yearbooks will help them to remember the people who were important to them and the events that took place in this period of their personal history.

In itself, this could be the most successful argument that can be made to convince students to take an interest in student publications. Perhaps that is why it is so important that student journalists cover all aspects of the academic environment, and that they remain oriented toward the people, events, and physical surroundings existing therein. Placing this material in context, in a historical record, is a service no others can perform.

Although the publications staff cannot expect to carry the complete burden of increasing school spirit and interest in student publications, significant contributions toward those goals can be made. If you face severe problems concerning these areas, do not expect quick results, as it may take a generation of students (3-4 years) to achieve more than minimal change. Work on the younger students served by the publications, and work on the younger teachers in the school system. These people are potentially your most supportive allies, and the more of them who are, the more likely it is that interest in the newspaper and yearbook will increase.

CHAPTER 28

Training Colleagues, Substitute Teachers, Parents, and News Sources to be Your Allies

In addition to the students who are not directly involved in the publications program, advisers often have difficulties with adults who do not have a financial stake in the publication. Some of the problems are associated with lack of interest, while others are caused by lack of understanding. Both causes require some action on your part if you desire a smooth operation.

Colleagues

The problems associated with colleagues generally are linked to their lack of interest, support, and understanding. By means of a vigorous campaign, however, some of these people can become the most avid supporters of the publication.

Although contributions may be solicited from your colleagues at the beginning of the school term, you probably will not receive many unless there is a follow up to the initial request with easy-to-complete monthly report forms, short surveys, and anonymous critique forms for the publication suggestion box. Give each teacher an ample supply of standardized forms, and on a separate sheet (not more than one page long) provide guidelines concerning exactly what you want to know. Whatever comments your colleagues make, do not criticize them or become overly defensive. Instead, try to build upon these comments. Additionally, when colleagues respond to your requests, acknowledge their responses with brief thank-you notes. Such action will increase the number of repeat performances.

Whenever there is the opportunity to do so, include "contribution reminders" in the administrative newsletters or weekly announcement bulletins that are circulated among your colleagues. The more times they see or hear such requests, the more likely they are to respond.

Staff meetings also provide good opportunities to make announcements requesting suggestions and support, but don't wait exclusively for such gatherings to make such needs known. Instead, suggest to the staff that on a weekly basis they informally talk to their teachers about newspaper or yearbook content. This will reinforce the idea that you are not the only person interested in their ideas.

On a more formal basis, to encourage your colleagues to complete the forms you create, assign teacher beats to the staff members so every teacher will be contacted at least once, well in advance of each deadline. Educate the staff members to collect monthly report forms and to scan the reports for clarity and completeness, as this is an important opportunity for your colleagues to publicize achievements of their students, activities of their classes, and news about the clubs they sponsor.

Additionally, creating a staff public relations position, as mentioned in earlier chapters, also serves the teacher-input needs and will be useful in supporting the high-visibility goals that have been set for the program. For example, when the staff engages in fund-raising activities to support the publications program, the public relations person should be in charge of informing all teachers about those activities.

Another tactic is to involve your colleagues indirectly with the publication process. If they sponsor clubs or organizations, ask them to make sure the groups each elect or appoint "correspondents" whose duty it is to convey to the staff information about group members and group activities. You may need to contact some sponsors and sell them on the idea that publicity (high visibility) for their groups is desirable. This tactic also works well on teachers who want to show that their "pet" classes are doing something worthwhile.

Other indirect involvement can be generated by requests that colleagues provide suggestions for journalism class writing assignments, provide information for a "teachers' section" in the publication, and announce publication sales in their classrooms. To promote the latter idea, provide teachers, if at all possible, with free copies of student newspapers and discount prices for yearbooks. They will feel much more positive about this task if they are provided with some kind of special treatment.

Although some of your colleagues will respond because of their own ego involvement with publicity, obtaining responses from other colleagues often is associated with gaining their overall support. This can be done in subtle ways and in direct ways.

One subtle way to gain support is by increasing awareness of the journalism program. To achieve this, you might post a deadline calendar in the faculty lounge, remain positive about the publications program whenever you talk with other teachers (no matter how much griping they do about their students), and invite them to visit the staff during production periods, so they can see what the staff does. Additionally, when publication activities are likely to disrupt other teachers' classes (e.g., during the periods when yearbook pictures are being taken), provide adequate and frequent reminders that such activities will be taking place. As a rule of thumb, instruct staff members not to disrupt other classes with publications activities.

A not-so-subtle way to gain support is to be supportive of other teachers by helping them out when assistance is needed. There are many minor tasks that can be done for others that will make them feel indebted to you, and this is important for times when the staff really needs something from them. You might even try to arrange teacher discounts on the package deals that yearbook photographers offer to their customers.

A variation of this theme is to directly arrange trade-offs between the publication staff and other classes. For example, staff photographers could take pictures and provide publicity for various classes and groups in exchange for illustrations for the publication (from art classes) or use of typewriters and computers (from the business department).

Overall, when dealing with colleagues, treat them as if you value their contributions and support, regardless of how poorly or insensitively they provide them. Eventually, they will be of help to the publication in one way or another, and in the process of encouraging them, you will help them to better understand the publications program. In terms of future dividends, that, in itself, is worthwhile.

Substitute Teachers

Unless substitute teachers are experienced in journalism, they generally will act as babysitters for the class unless they are directed to do something specific. While this may be acceptable in some classes, when your staff has a deadline to meet, they cannot afford to lose many days during the publication cycle. A brief absence on your part may not disrupt the cycle, especially if the "lost days" described in earlier chapters have been built into the production calender, but there is no need to automatically lose time when you are absent. With correct planning, any teacher can be taught to keep the publication wheels turning.

The major problems concerning substitute teachers will stem from their lack of understanding of journalism. Substitute teachers who are not experienced in journalism often will not understand the necessities of the operation, and therefore they will inadvertently cause problems by enforcing traditional classroom behavior. To avoid such problems, create a permanent list of guidelines that substitute teachers may consult. The guidelines should be left with the administrator responsible for dealing with the substitute teachers, and they should indicate the quirks associated with publication production, so the replacements won't expect staff members to remain quietly in their seats for the entire period.

The guidelines also should list the locations of equipment and materials most likely to be needed in your absence, and the names of responsible students that substitutes could trust to give reliable answers to questions concerning policy and procedure. Most often, these students would be editors who would know what had to be done and how to do it, if deadline time was near. Preparing sets of writing review exercises for students not involved in the immediate production aspects also is a useful step to take.

For times when the staff is not on deadline and you know you will be absent for only a day, prepare a list of journalism-related discussion questions that almost any educated adult could handle. Include several variations on each theme that a question introduces, so the substitutes can see possible directions for discussion.

Also, prepare a long-term "substitutes' survival kit" for times when your absence is prolonged, whether it is planned or not. Give this kit to the administrator who deals with substitutes. In addition to the contents noted above, this kit should contain the names and telephone numbers of people and companies with whom the journalism program does business, brief descriptions of the functions these people and businesses serve, and complete projections about the content of and the deadlines for forthcoming publications. Copies of lesson plans also should be included in the long-term kit.

Parents

Parents, like the students who are not involved in journalism, will not care very much about the school's journalism program. Oddly enough, this is true even of the parents of most students who are involved in the program. To combat their lack of support, try to educate them about high school journalism.

If you divide the parents into two groups, those whose children are enrolled in journalism and those whose children are not, it will be easy to divide your "parental support engagement" energies appropriately. Work directly on the parents whose children are enrolled in journalism and indirectly on the others.

One effective tactic that will gain support from the parents of journalism students is to invite them to various activities. For example, at the beginning of the school year, try to arrange either an open house for them at school or meet with them and their children (your staff members) at a time convenient for everyone. At whatever gathering that can be arranged, provide a short presentation about journalism. Take this opportunity to explain the benefits of journalism training and the demands that will be made during the year. The presentation should reinforce information that you might already have sent to parents in conjunction with contracts they and their children were asked to sign (see chapter 3).

Parents also can be invited to visit your classroom, either as observers or as resource people. Many parents have skills relevant to a journalism operation, and if their schedules permit, they may be willing to share such skills with the staff members. Other invitations might involve opportunities to chaperon field trips and supervise fund-raising activities, or on a more personal basis, to write guest editorials or be featured in one way or another.

Finally, at the end of the school year, arrange a journalism banquet for staff members and their parents. Keep the cost to a minimum, as that will attract more participants, and take the opportunity to summarize the year's accomplishments and to thank parents for their cooperation.

Some indirect methods that can be used to assist in gaining support from the students' parents include helping them out by providing transportation for their children whenever publication activities require after-hours work, sending them thank-you notes for the use of their children (this always surprises parents), and sending them positive information about their children's progress. As often as possible, use newsletters that parents receive from the school district to convey information about the journalism program.

Although you should not worry much about the parents of children not enrolled in journalism, there are some things that can be done to keep journalism on their minds, too. For instance, in the material that is placed in school district newsletters to parents, include some general information about the journalism program. Additionally, send them questionnaires, if possible, which ask for their suggestions about student publications. Finally, suggest to your staff to include a "parents' corner" in the school newspaper, to increase parental interest in the publication.

Ultimately, remember that there will not be an overwhelming response to any of these tactics used to increase parental support for journalism, but don't be discouraged by this. All the things that you attempt will have a cumulative effect on some parents, and sometime, somehow, the program will benefit from them.

News Sources

News sources are students, teachers, administrators, and members of the public who contribute information to student publications, and most of the problems they will cause will flow from their misunderstandings about journalistic operation. Either they will not provide enough information or they will provide too much information, and some will be unhappy with whatever coverage the students provide them. Because they do not understand the newsgathering and editing processes, they will miss deadlines and react negatively to any editing of the information they provide.

Fortunately, repeated use of the same news sources improves their relationship with the program, as they soon will learn what to expect and what is expected of them. Do all you can to educate them about the process, and that may mean creating a brief statement that explains what the staff members will be doing all year long in terms of interviews and editing.

Post the statement and distribute it to all school personnel at the beginning of the school year, making it clear that deadlines are important, that material will be edited, and that mistakes will be made. Thank them in advance for their understanding, and ask them for their indulgence in the staffs' learning process. This is all that can be done, in addition to your other public relations contacts, to assuage the anguish of news sources.

After reading this chapter, you may think that dealing with colleagues, substitute teachers, parents, and news sources will take all of your energies. Although they seem like monumental tasks, once some headway has been made, the tasks shrink in comparison to your efforts to deal with staff members and their publications. The initial efforts may be overwhelming at first, but after the processes have been set in motion, less and less time will be required to nuture the momentum resulting from your work. Ultimately, an occasional assist from you will be necessary, but the effort will not consume you. In fact, after the first year of practice, assists will become second nature.

CHAPTER 29
Motivating Community Business Owners and Managers

If you have ever tried to convince the owner of a local business to purchase advertising in a student publication, you may already know how hard it is to gain such support. Although some community businesses are eager to contribute to the success of student newspapers and yearbooks, many find that their advertising interests are better served through the professional mass media. This is especially true when student groups from various schools in a community saturate businesses with requests for financial support.

While your students may be up against a good deal of competition for the local advertising dollar, student publication staffs have several advantages over other groups requesting funds. If these advantages are used to their fullest extent, the staff members' campaign can yield more than money.

Increasing Awareness

To increase support from community businesses, the students must show the owners that advertising in a student publication is worthwhile. One way to do this is to conduct a student survey to determine which businesses students patronize. Survey results can then be shared with the competitors of those businesses that faired well in the survey.

Even if the staff does not conduct a survey, making a list of the ways students support community businesses can be an effective way to convince local business owners to support student publications. A generic list of spending habits can be a forceful reminder that teenagers are a major market for many retailers.

Another type of awareness that needs to be promoted by the staff is the awareness that a school publication actually exists. If the only time business owners have contact with student publications is when staff members solicit money, they are not likely to have a favorable impression of student publications. The staff can combat this image by subtly expanding business-related content.

For example, the staff could publish alumni updates, which might focus on former students who have become successful locally. Also, suggest that publications include newsworthy material about local business leaders, or content contributed by them, e.g., guest columns concerning relevant topics. In either case, such publicity makes it harder for businesses not to support student publications.

Other techniques involve direct action by local business leaders. One technique is to invite local business owners to address the staff about relevant topics. Another is to request that local businesses display posters promoting student publications and their public activities, such as fund-raising events. A third method is to give small numbers of student newspapers to selected businesses for distribution to customers. Each of these methods raises business leaders' awareness of student publications, creates the perception thet such publications are performing a community service, and reduces the business community's resistance to later requests for supporting funds.

Advertising Deals

When it comes right down to selling advertisements to local business owners, staff members can make a common business deal look very attractive. First, if the publication uses photographs, help the students create prototype advertisements using pictures. This technique frequently improves the selling success rate. Be aware, however, that this technique often requires large amounts of time.

Additionally, create advertising package deals that no local business owners could refuse. Offer cut-rate packages (e.g., six ads for half of what six single ads would normally cost), larger ads for the price of smaller ads (if the business buys a series), or any other incentive that can be created. You might even negotiate some kind of trade-off that could supply the staff with needed materials at less expense, which might result in a tax break for the business.

The Final Process

After convincing local business owners to give some financial support to student publications, make certain a signed contract is obtained if money is involved. Unfortunately, some people are happy to buy advertising until the bill comes, and thus some of the problems with community businesses will result from lack of payment for advertising. When this happens, you may have to visit the business owner in person to collect. If there is a problem collecting payment, do not be satisfied to talk to a secretary or clerk in the accounting office of the business involved. Speak directly to the owner or person who signed the contract. In extreme cases, ask the school's attorney to call, but avoid such action if at all possible.

Along with the bills the publication advertising manager sends, include thank-you notes for the support the staff has received. This step is a very important one, and it should neither be neglected nor treated insufficiently. Consider creating certificates of acknowledgment for businesses that contribute significantly or consistently to student publications, for such certificates, when framed, could be public relations devices for both a business and a publication.

In general, the relationship between community businesses and student publications is affected in the same ways relationships between people-at-large and student publications are affected. There needs to be awareness and incentive, and there is overlap among all parties involved. For example, parents are in some cases business owners; business owners are sometimes alumni; and alumni are sometimes members of the PTA. Any awareness of student publications that can be instilled in any of these people, whether it is through personal contact or not, will have some positive effect on their relationship with the publication. Seize every opportunity for publicity and incentive, and milk it for all it's worth.

CHAPTER 30
Keeping Outside Production Personnel at Their Best

Most frequently, problems with professionals in the publishing business will occur in relationship to yearbook production, although problems with typesetters or printers also could affect student newspapers that are typeset or printed professionally. Generally, such problems arise when the staff's needs are not met, so it must be certain that the professionals with whom you deal know exactly what is expected of them. Contingency plans must also be devised for quickly solving whatever problems these people might cause.

Typesetters

Problems most often associated with typesetters involve their failure to follow directions, produce satisfactory work, and meet deadlines. Frequently, these problems are not entirely the fault of the typesetters, as publication staff members are not overly skilled in providing the information necessary to avoid the problems.

When a typesetter has been decided upon, either through a bidding process, a recommendation process, or some combination of both, arrange a meeting with the person in charge of the account and learn about the company's operating system. Ask for samples of all the fonts (typestyles) available to the publication staff, a type-counting guide for the fonts the staff will most likely use (so they can accurately estimate the length of copy and headlines), and a list of typesetter's marks used by the company (so your staff can mark copy appropriately). Also ask about the company's pickup and delivery system (for moving copy between your school and the company) and the turn-around time for typesetting copy (one or two working days is reasonable, unless you send an enormous amount at one time).

Once you and your staff know exactly what you are dealing with, in terms of managing and marking copy, all of you will be much better equipped to avoid author errors (mistakes caused by those who mark copy inappropriately). Author errors result in "redos," lost time, and extra cost. Learning to avoid author errors may take hours of study and a lot of practice, but it is well worth any time and energy the copy editors can spend on it.

As you might guess, author errors cause unsatisfactory work and missed deadlines, but they are not the only causes of these problems. Sometimes, typesetters are careless and disorganized, and can themselves create unsatisfactory work and miss deadlines. For example, typeset copy from the printer might contain a lot of typographical errors or be printed too lightly. If this happens, in a friendly, diplomatic way, demand that it be redone without charge. Most reputable typesetters won't even send this kind of work, and they will, without question, accommodate reasonable requests from their customers.

To avoid involvement with typesetters who frequently send out inferior work or who are reluctant to redo inferior work without charge, check their references before making arrangements to send the publications work to them. Also, if possible, tour their facilities and find out their system of checking work, e.g., find out how many times completed copy is checked by someone other than the person doing the typesetting.

If you are stuck with a typesetter who causes problems, act immediately to alleviate those problems. Personal visits to the head of the company may be necessary, especially if it is a small company. Otherwise, begin working your way up the chain of command, but don't be put off by employees who cannot be of help. Be persistent, for the service being provided costs money, no matter how sloppy it is.

Printers

Unless you work with a very small printing operation, the publication will be assigned a publisher's representative who will handle all dealings with the printing company, once the contract is signed. To ensure that satisfactory service will be received from the representative, the contract should include the minimal number of visits the representative will make to the school, the approximate schedule of such visits, and the number and type of mini-workshops the representative will conduct for the staff concerning aspects of the printing process. It is important to have these specifications in writing so there is some leverage in meeting the staffs' needs.

It also is important to gain a reputation for taking printing bids every year, as this procedure helps to keep publisher representatives from taking the account for granted. In fact, before signing any printing contract, ask each company that bids on the contract for a list of educational customers that it serves in the area. Then, contact those customers and ask them about the company's performance record. Eventually, word will spread through the publishing grapevine that you check references, which will protect the program from being seen as an "easy mark."

If you have joined a regional or national press association, it should be easy to obtain from other members their evaluations of various regional or national printing companies. At the very least, if you are not familiar with the quality of service these companies provide, contact other advisers in the area to find out about their experiences with printers. Do this even if it only means finding out whether or not a company has a toll-free telephone number for its customers.

Once a contract has been signed, act with an air of confidence, as you really are the boss in your association with a printer's representative. If you are reserved or timid in your dealings with this person, you may not obtain all you could receive, including personal service and cost-cutting advice. In other words, a seasoned representative might take advantage of the publication, either because of laziness or greed.

To keep everybody honest, keep in constant touch with the representative, and keep a running list of questions to ask during each contact. It is especially important that time is not wasted when a representative visits the school, and the list of questions will allow the representative to begin work immediately upon arrival. When arranging a visit, make certain to schedule it for a time when both you and the staff are available, i.e., not during deadline time and not at a time when the staff can't be present.

When the representative does a good job or does something beyond your expectations, show this appreciation by letting the company know about your satisfaction. Such action will encourage good relations between you and your representative.

On the other hand, if the representative fails to meet certain needs, immediately make your dissatisfaction known. First, try to work out the problems with the representative, and keep meticulous records of the complaints and the attempts to resolve them.

If your one-on-one approach does not succeed, let the school administration know there are problems and that you plan to contact the representative's supervisor. When calling the printing company, do not be satisfied to talk with a secretary or some other person without power over your representative; talk to the representative's superior. Specify exactly what it will take to rectify the situation, and if necessary, provide this person with written documentation of the problems that were encountered.

Ultimately, if satisfaction cannot be obtained from either your representative or the printing company, consider dropping this company from the list of potential bidders, which in effect eliminates it from bidding on future contracts. If this step is taken, notify the president of the company and include an explanation for the action that is being taken. The results that such letters have are sometimes amazing.

Photographers

Like printers, photographers need to be told exactly what is expected of them (in terms of both picture size and deadlines), and they should be made to bid on the photography contract every year. There are several national firms that send photography teams throughout the country to take yearbook pictures, so there is no reason to feel trapped into using a local firm if its past performance or prices are not satisfactory. Often, national firms can offer better prices and more options than local firms, merely because of the size of their operation.

Again, it is wise to obtain information about photographers who have served other schools, to help in choosing a company that will satisfy publication needs. Be sure to ask about promptness and quality of service, both in terms of physical service (when the pictures are taken and when they are delivered) and technical service (quality of pictures and number of options).

Additionally, some personal training in photography would enable you to know what you are talking about when you discuss various photographic options. If you cannot take a course in photography, at least arrange to spend some time with a professional photographer, either at the local newspaper or at a professional portrait studio.

If you choose a local photographer without any kind of regional or national reputation, keep in constant touch with him or her, send reminders concerning deadlines, and specify in writing what you expect. Be sure to make the photographer feel appreciated, as this will help you obtain what you need.

When problems do arise, try to solve them immediately. Remember that the printing deadlines often will be linked to photography deadlines, so you cannot afford delays in solving photography problems. Try to work out the problems with the photography company, but if satisfaction is not obtained, go to the administration for help. In your contacts with the company, remember to insist on talking to someone with power; secretaries often are trained to shield their bosses from complaints, and thus if you do not speak directly to someone with decision-making power, the problem may not be solved in time to meet other deadlines.

When dealing with a local photographer, the principal or the school board probably will have more influence than you will have in forcing the photographer to do what the contract requires. Do not, however, expect miracles from local photographers who may have cornered the photography market in small communities.

Probably the most effective step that can be taken to gain satisfaction from a local photographer is to explain to that person the importance of the publication to the students and the school administration. Also, note the printing deadlines that are linked to the photographic deadlines, and if all else fails, remind your photographer that other firms would be happy to have your business.

In spite of all your efforts, printers and professional photographers will still manage to thwart the operation in one way or another. Some will do it intentionally, for their own gain or convenience, but most will do it because you have not made clear what is expected of them. Take the time to learn about printing and photography so you can specify exactly what you want, and include those specifications in the contracts. Once this is done, the main job will be to see that the specifications are met.

CHAPTER 31

Dealing with Natural Disasters and Human-Produced Disasters

One of the most depressing aspects of publications advising is to see the staffs' efforts hindered or destroyed by one disaster or another. Natural disasters, such as fires, tornadoes, floods, and weather-related accidents, may cause more destruction than human-produced disasters, but sometimes the latter type of disaster can be more devastating because of its preventable nature. Regardless of the type of disaster with which you must cope, life will be easier if you know what to do before and after a disaster occurs.

Natural Disasters

Before a natural disaster strikes, treat student production materials as you would treat valuables at home: store them in a safe place, such as a fireproof, waterproof safe. This is especially true for picture negatives, copies of completed pages, and small pieces of valuable equipment such as cameras and their accessories. When possible, take home duplicate copies of written work, and tell staff members to take home duplicate copies of any work they complete.

Another preventive measure is to document everything that will be used in the production process, by creating a detailed list of equipment, including cost, serial numbers (if appropriate), and dates of purchase. This information will help expedite insurance claims during the replacement process. Additionally, whenever you mail material to your typographer or printer, keep photocopies of the originals and send the materials via registered mail, so there will be a record for Postal Service traces, if necessary.

When a natural disaster does destroy publication materials, there are several steps that can be taken to salvage the situation. For example, if negatives and pictures of important events are destroyed, ask amateur photographers and photographers from the local newspaper or rival schools (all of whom might have covered the events) to share their negatives with the staff. The local paper and rival schools may allow the use of their photographs and copy, if the staff's stories describing the events are irreplaceable. If photocopies of completed pages have been kept, it should be relatively easy to reproduce them, even if different pictures have to be used.

To combat disasters that merely hinder a staff's work instead of destroying it, e.g., weather that closes the school for extended periods of time, be sure the staff completes work well in advance of deadlines. This is another good reason for creating false deadlines for the staff.

Sometimes a natural disaster occurs outside of the area under your control, such as at the site of the printing company that has a set of the staff's completed flats. If such a disaster does occur, the staff will be prepared by having kept duplicates or copies of the materials that were sent for processing.

The natural disaster that is the most difficult to cope with is the death of a staff member, but as mentioned in earlier chapters, if staff members have been cross-trained, the operation should be able to continue without much physical disruption. The emotional disruption, however, may be a large problem, so be prepared to play psychologist for the remaining staff members, even if they receive professional help from others.

Human-Produced Disasters

Generally, the kinds of disasters that can be avoided are the human-produced ones, which include such things as breaking, losing or misusing equipment, or destroying materials. Unfortunately, while you can limit this type of behavior on the part of the staff, you have little control over it where others are concerned.

In order to prevent staff members from breaking, losing, or misusing their equipment, instill in them the idea that camera equipment, word-processing equipment, and typesetting equipment is delicate and must be treated with great care. They also should be made aware of the costs of such items, so that they know exactly how much money it will take to replace them.

Another preventive measure to take is to thoroughly educate the staff members who will be using delicate equipment. They should be trained to operate the equipment and to care for it properly. All members of the staff, whether they will be using the equipment or not, should be told not to eat, drink, or smoke around it, as the possibility for disaster increases immensely when these elements are introduced into the situation. This rule also should be strictly enforced in any room in which production takes place, to avoid accidental destruction of completed copy and pictures.

To keep equipment from "disappearing," create and enforce check-out procedures so that you will know where each piece of equipment is at all times. This is an especially valuable technique for keeping track of photography equipment, which many advisers find to have "legs of its own." Consider appointing an equipment manager who, along with you, will have one of the few keys to the safe where camera equipment is kept.

If a human-produced disaster occurs outside of your area of control, demand compensation from those responsible. For example, if the printing company delays the distribution by sending the publications to some other school, misprints the yearbooks or newspapers, or ruins other materials, calculate and insist upon receipt of a reasonable dollar amount to compensate the staff members for their anguish or extra work. It would be good to include in publication contracts a clause that would cover such a situation.

Whenever any disaster delays distribution of the staff's publication, the publication's audience should be informed as soon as possible concerning the causes of the delay and the steps being taken to alleviate the situation. If, in the case of a delayed yearbook, distribution will take place after the school year ends, arrangements for distribution should be made before the close of school, to avoid confusion and further delays. If direct mailing from the printing plant is desired, and if circumstances warrant it, mailing charges should be collected in advance.

While some disasters are preventable, not all are completely avoidable. With a moderate amount of foresight, you can predict most human-produced disasters, and you can compensate for most natural disasters. Advisers must try to do both.

CHAPTER 32

Adding Computers to Your Program

As high school journalism moves into the age of technology and desktop publishing, advisers nationwide are considering numerous equipment options for their publication staffs. Most of these decisions are limited by lack of knowledge and lack of financial resources, but before electronic publishing in the classroom is rejected, advisers should look at the benefits that can be realized when staff members are able to typeset their own yearbooks and newspapers.

Lack of Knowledge

Whatever decisions you reach about preparing to enter the age of electronic publishing, obtain plenty of information about available possibilities. This may be done in several ways.

First, obtain the names, addresses, and toll-free telephone numbers of companies that sell electronic publishing equipment. Most large libraries have computer-oriented magazines, in which these companies are listed. Call or write to these companies, explain the needs of the publication, and request information and brochures concerning what the companies have to offer. Be sure to ask for price quotations, as many brochures do not mention equipment costs.

After studying the brochures and choosing perhaps two or three systems that will suit the publication, obtain from the corresponding companies the names and telephone numbers of people and schools who are using such systems. Contact these people and question them about the advantages and disadvantages of the system they are using. People are generally happy to share information of this nature with others who are seeking advice. If possible, personally observe systems in operation. Through inquiries and observations, you may find that what you thought was the best system actually is too complicated for staff members to learn quickly, or that it doesn't do all a salesperson said it would do.

Also, be wary of creating or purchasing a system that mixes components from different manufacturers. While such systems sometimes work well, there is a good possibility they will contain "glitches" (errors in the system that cause malfunctions), which many computer service representatives will blame on the components not manufactured by their employers. This means you may never get rid of the glitches.

Lack of Finances

In well-populated schools where thick yearbooks are ordered in large numbers, a desktop publishing system can easily pay for itself well within its lifetime. The savings that are realized in charges for typesetting and special graphics amount to thousands of dollars over a relatively short term, and when similar savings of newspaper typesetting charges are added in, the break-even period becomes even shorter.

Advisers really should analyze their typesetting and graphics costs, and then they should compare such amounts to the pro-rated annual cost of a desktop publishing system (over its projected lifetime). Although the initial investment might seem enormous, in terms of what an adviser or school system may be used to, the long-term savings may make such an investment worthwhile.

If a new system costs too much, look into the possibility of purchasing a reconditioned system, or at least part of either a new or used system. If nothing else, you might be able to purchase the front end of a system (the video display terminals and computer disk drives) that is compatible with the typesetting system used by the publication's current typesetter. This would at least allow the staff more freedom to create layouts that will work successfully the first time. It also would be the first step in what might become a series of purchases that would eventually eliminate the need for an outside typesetter.

Of course, arrangements with the current typesetting company to typeset what the staff members create on their disks should be made well in advance of any such purchase. Otherwise, you may be left with a front-end system and no access to typesetting and printing.

Benefits

One of the immediate benefits associated with in-house typesetting is the reduction of mental anguish that accompanies publication production. When students are able to typeset their own material, they can save time in designing layouts and they can meet deadlines more efficiently. This is true because they not only can judge immediately whether or not a story will fit in the allotted space, but they can correct typesetting errors in a matter of minutes, instead of the days it sometimes requires when an outside firm is used.

Overall, the publication will contain fewer errors and will look better for two reasons: 1) the staff will spend less time trying to fix something that didn't come back from the typesetter quite as they had expected, and 2) they will spend more time correcting errors that normally would have slipped by for reasons of convenience. These improvements, in themselves, will reduce the mental stress that always accompanies that part of the process.

Another result of these freedoms is that you and the staff members will be less stressed by the typesetting functions that need to be completed and the typesetting schedules that need to be met. In fact, in "emergencies," the staff could have access to typesetting equipment on weekends and evenings, when other typesetting businesses would normally be closed. Additionally, staff members will have more time to improve other aspects of the publication, such as the writing of material being typeset.

A final benefit of owning your own typesetting equipment is that the student journalists will receive hands-on training that makes them competitive with other high school journalists who pursue journalism beyond high school. In college, former staff members will have to compete with other students for positions on the student newspaper or yearbook, and those with typesetting experience are more likely to obtain paid staff positions. Financial assistance of this nature might be the critical difference that allows a student to afford higher education.

Similarly, in the professional world, when the students apply for part-time jobs at the local paper or other local publishing companies, their chances of success are greatly enhanced if they have typesetting skills. With the increasing number of high schools involved in electronic publishing of one variety or another, the program really needs to move in this direction (if it hasn't already done so) if staff members are to gain skills comparable to those held by their job market competition.

While the process of selecting and using an electronic publishing system may look ominous at first, once you become involved you will find that the joys far outnumber the sorrows. If you talk with people who own such computer systems, you will find that this is true. The caveats mentioned above are not designed to discourage your investment in a computer system. On the contrary, they should serve as guideposts as you make your way down the electronic publishing road.

CHAPTER 33

Distributing the Publication

Before the staff has completed work on the publication, some arrangements should be made to distribute it. Systems of distribution usually vary according to the type and cost of the publication, and the cooperation advisers can obtain from their colleagues. Often, some form of interaction between both elements determines the amount of chaos associated with distribution.

Newspapers Versus Yearbooks

Newspapers are almost always easier to distribute than yearbooks, whether or not students must pay for their copies. In schools where newspapers are free, the easiest method of distribution is to place the papers in designated spots near high-traffic pedestrian areas such as main entries to school buildings or to the school cafeteria. A more enterprising method of distribution, which requires a bit more time and manpower coordination, is to leave a certain number of papers in front of each classroom door before first period classes. This method works best if papers can be placed above the floor in noticeable positions.

When there is a charge for newspapers, a group of sales people (perhaps working on commission) should be ready to sell papers before school and during lunch. Each salesperson should be given a designated number of papers and a designated amount of change, so proper accounting can take place. The price of a newspaper should be kept as low as possible, and appropriate denominations of change should be available to staff members who sell the publication. Papers available to students at reduced cost through subscription should be picked up in the journalism room, and a staff member should check off the name of each subscriber on the subscription list who picks up a copy.

One note of caution is that the entire school staff should be notified in advance when staff members will be distributing newspapers, as students have a tendency to read school newspapers during class periods, which often can be very disruptive.

Yearbooks, which seldom are free, pose a different set of problems because their bulk prevents them from being distributed easily in several locations, and they cannot be distributed randomly if they are personalized, e.g., if they have students' names embossed on them. The best technique involves publicizing the times when yearbooks will be distributed, sufficiently staffing the distribution area, and being organized. Distribution should be done by using several periods during two or three days, if the number of people ordering yearbooks is quite large.

Ask that those who have purchased yearbooks in advance, which should be most of those interested in them, have their receipts and some form of identification ready when they come to pick up their copies. The staff should have some form of duplicate receipt system and an alphabetical master list of those who have ordered. Matching receipts and checking off names should then be quite easy, and most of the distribution time will be spent checking identification of those students whom the staff does not know on sight.

Cooperation From Colleagues

When colleagues support student publications, distribution becomes significantly easier because, within reasonable limits, the distribution process will have more freedom to disrupt classes for the sake of efficiency. For example, when newspapers are free, teachers may be willing to distribute them in their classrooms. When there is a charge for newspapers, teachers may allow a salesperson to take 10 minutes of class time to sell papers, or they may even be willing to sell papers at the end of their last class.

Cooperative colleagues may be just as helpful where yearbook distribution is concerned, although the help probably will come in the form of giving their students time off from class to pick up yearbooks. Traditionally, students who receive yearbooks read them immediately and exchange them with friends for the purposes of signing. On yearbook distribution day, some schools designate times during which such activities may be carried out without penalty and without uncontrolled disruption of classwork. A good idea would be to arrange for such a period well in advance of when the yearbooks arrive from the printing company.

Overall, well-organized distribution systems operate smoothly, with or without the cooperation of others. Part of a good system, as mentioned earlier, is good publicity. Another part is consistency; for example, it is particularly good to distribute newspapers repeatedly in the same way, in the same places. Finally, the staff members should know in advance that they are expected to help with distribution. This will save you from seeking outside help and having to pay sales commissions.

A Final Note — What You Can Do To Help

Although this handbook presents literally hundreds of ideas for dealing with problems that confront high school journalism advisers, there always is room for improvement. If you have encountered a problem that is not covered generally or specifically by this handbook, if you have a solution that has not been mentioned concerning a problem that the handbook does address, or if you have any other suggestion for improving the handbook, jot it down and send it to either of the following addresses:

Dr. Bruce L. Plopper
Department of Journalism
2801 S. University Avenue
University of Arkansas at Little Rock
Little Rock, AR 72204

or

Quill and Scroll Society
School of Journalism & Mass Communication
The University of Iowa
Iowa City, IA 52242

Your contributions will be carefully considered for inclusion in future editions of the handbook, so that others may benefit from your experience. Don't hesitate to write; we're all in this together.

SECTION V
GUIDES TO RESOURCES

Organizations Relevant to High School Journalism

American Newspaper Publishers Association Foundation
The Newspaper Center
Box 17407
Dulles International Airport
Washington, DC 20041

Offers single, free copies of the pamphlets, *Newspaper Jobs You Never Thought Of ... Or Did You?* and *How to apply for a Job in Media* and *Newspapers ... Your Future?* Also offers for $1.00, *The Anatomy of a Newspaper* booklet. Publishes a Newspaper in Education (NIE) bibliography of works which deal with using newspapers in education or developing language skills. Publishes *NIE Update* monthly. Offers workshops for teachers.

American Scholastic Press Association
Box 563
Wheatley Heights, NY 11798

Offers awards and reviews scholastic publications.

The Business Press Educational Foundation, Inc.
675 Third Avenue
New York, NY 10017-5704

Offers case study materials for schools and brochures on careers in the business press. Arranges speakers, and faculty and student internships.

Columbia Scholastic Press Association
Box 11
Central Mail Room
Columbia University
New York, NY 10027-6969

Offers "Gold Circle Awards" to student journalists through its rating service for high school publications. Evaluates student yearbooks, magazines, newspapers; offers contests and publicatications. Conducts a convention in November for yearbook staffs and advisers and a convention in March for all publications staffs and advisers as well as a summer workshop. Publishes the *Student Press Review* periodical.

C-SPAN In The Classroom
P.O. Box 75298
Washington, DC 20013

Offers an "Educator's Kit" including guides to C-Span programming.

Dow Jones Newspaper Fund, Inc.
P.O. Box 300
Princeton, NJ 08540-0300

Gives grants for high school journalism workshops for minorities; offers free, single copies of a journalism career and scholarship guide.

Journalism Education Association
Kedzie Hall 104
Kansas State University
Manhattan, KS 66506-1501

An organization of journalism teachers and publications advisers, which publishes two magazines: *Communication: Journalism Education Today* and *Newswire*. Offers conventions for educators and advisers, contests for students, scholarships for high school journalists, and hotline help for advisers.

National Newspaper Association
Suite 400
1627 K Street, N.W.
Washington, DC 20006

Offers the pamphlets, *Journalism: Your Newspaper Career and How to Prepare for it* and *To A Rewarding Career in Journalism.*

National Press Photographers Association, Inc.
Charles H. Cooper, Executive Director
3200 Croasdaile Drive, Suite 306
Durham, NC 27705

Offers the pamphlet, *Careers in News Photography.*

National Scholastic Press Association
620 Rarig Center
330 21st Ave. South
University of Minnesota
Minneapolis, MN 55455

Evaluates student yearbooks, magazines, and newspapers; offers contests, scholarships, guidebooks, and awards. Holds an annual high school press convention in the fall and spring in addition to summer workshops. Lends copies of award-winning yearbooks and newspapers. Produces *Trends* periodical about high school publications.

New England School Press Association
College of Journalism
Northeastern University
Boston, MA 02115

The Poynter Institute for Media Studies
801 Third Street South
St. Petersburg, FL 33701

Offers seminars for journalism teachers and publishes *Best Newspaper Writing*, which is a collection of newspaper work judged to be finalists and winners of the American Society of Newspaper Editors Distinguished Writing Awards

Quill and Scroll Society
School of Journalism and Mass Communication
The University of Iowa
Iowa City, IA 52242-1089

An international honorary society for high school journalists, Quill and Scroll publishes *Quill & Scroll* magazine. Offers international writing and photo contests open to all students, and a news media evaluation and yearbook excellence contest open to member schools only. Offers various inexpensive publications and awards related to high school journalism.

Radio-Television News Directors Association
100 Connecticut Ave. N.W., Suite 615
Washington, DC 20036

Offers *Careers in Broadcast News*, a free pamphlet. Publishes a monthly magazine, *The RTNDA Communicator*, and a bi-weekly newsletter, *Intercom*. Provides names of local members to interested students.

Secondary Education Division
Association for Education in Journalism
  and Mass Communication
College of Journalism
University of South Carolina
Columbia, SC 29208

Conducts research concerning high school journalism and offers educational programs in conjunction with the AEJMC annual convention in August and the mid-winter conference during January.

Society of Professional Journalists
P. O. Box 77
Greencastle, IN 46135-0077

Dedicated to preserving a free and unfettered press, stimulating high standards and ethical behavior in the practice of journalism. Offers career information; publishes *Quill* magazine which contains timely topics on press issues,, ethics, etc.

Southern Interscholastic Press Association
College of Journalism
University of South Carolina
Columbia, SC 29208

Offers workshops, contests, and conventions. Provides critique service and awards for yearbooks, magazines, broadcast journalism, and newspapers.

Southern Regional Press Institute
Mass Communications Program
Savannah State College
Savannah, GA 31404

Conducts annual two-day workshop for high school journalism students and advisers.

Student Editors Association
504 S. Wheaton Ave.
Wheaton, IL 60187

Student Press Law Center
1735 Eye Street, NW, Suite 504
Washington, DC 20006-2402
(202) 466-5242

Serves as a national legal aid agency providing legal assistance and information to students and faculty advisers experiencing censorship or other legal problems. Publishes the *Student Press Law Center Report*.

Suburban Newspapers of America
111 E. Wacker Dr.
Chicago, IL 60601

Offers a free brochure titled, *Suburban Newspaper Careers*.

Women in Communications, Inc.
2101 Wilson Blvd., Suite 417
Arlington, VA 22201

Offers free, single copies of *Careers in Communications*.

Youth Communication
Suite 200,, 1320 18th St. N.W.
Washington, DC 20036-1811

Sponsors a network of large-circulation, youth-written newspapers and news bureaus in cities across the United States and Canada and a North American-wide news service covering youth issues. Offers a Youth News Service (YNS) which is a news cooperative for youth and community newspapers, much like the Associated Press for commercial newspapers.

Publications Useful to High School Journalism Advisers

Design and Production

Craig, James. *Basic Typography: A Design Manual (A Manual for Designers, Non-Designers & Desktop Publishers)*. New York: Watson-Guptill, 1990.

_____. *Production for the Graphic Designer*. Second ed.; New York: Watson-Guptill, 1990.

Crow, Wendell C. *Communication Graphics*. Englewood Cliffs, N.J.: Prentice-Hall, 1986.

Finberg, Howard I., and Bruce D. Itule. *Visual Editing: A Graphic Guide for Journalists*. Belmont, Calif: Wadsworth, Inc., 1990.

Garcia, Mario. *Contemporary Newspaper Design: A Structural Approach*. Second ed.; Englewood Cliffs, N.J.: Prentice-Hall, 1987.

Kruse, Benedict. *Desktop Publishing: Producing Professional Publications*. Albany, N.Y.: Delmar, 1989.

Lattimore, Dan, and Art Terry. *Desktop Publishing Study Guide*. Englewood, Colo.: Morton Publishing Co., 1990.

Moen, Daryl R. *Newspaper Layout and Design*. Second ed.; Ames, Iowa: Iowa State University Press, 1989.

Nelson, Roy Paul. *Publication Design*. Fifth ed.; Dubuque, Iowa: Wm. C. Brown, 1991.

High School Journalism

Abrams, J. Marc, and Michael Simpson. *Law of the Student Press*. Iowa City, Iowa: Quill and Scroll 1992.

Adams, Julian, and Kenneth Stratton. *Press Time*. Fourth ed.; Englewood Cliffs, N.J.: Prentice-Hall, Inc., 1985.

Bard, Rachel. *Newswriting Guide: A Handbook for Student Reporters*. Second ed.; Tacoma, Wash.: The Writer's Helpers, 1988.

Black, Jim N. *Managing the Student Yearbook: A Resource for Modern Yearbook Management and Design*. Dallas, Texas: Taylor Publishing Co., 1983.

Bond, Serena K. *Basic Skills School Newspaper Workbook*. Jonesboro, Ark.: ESP, 1983.

_____. *The School Newspaper*. Jonesboro, Ark.: ESP, 1982.

Button, Robert. *Managing Publications*. Iowa City, Iowa: Quill and Scroll 1982.

Dubrovnin, Vivian. *Running a School Newspaper*. Danbury, Conn.: Franklin Watts, Inc., 1985.

Engel, Jackie, ed. *Survival Kit for School Publication Advisers*. Fifth ed.; Lawrence, Kansas: Kansas Scholastic Press Association, School of Journalism, University of Kansas, 1990.

English, Earl, Clarence Hach, and Tom Rolnicki. *Scholastic Journalism*. Eighth ed.; Ames, Iowa: Iowa State University Press, 1990.

Ferguson, Donald L., and Jim Patton. *Journalism Today: an Introduction*. Lincolnwood, Ill.: National Textbook Co., 1986.

Garcia, Mario. *The New Adviser*. Second ed.; New York: Columbia Scholastic Press Association, 1978.

Gilmore, Gene. *Inside High School Journalism*. Glenview, Ill.: Scott, Foresman and Company, 1986.

Greenman, Robert. *The Adviser's Companion*. New York: Columbia Scholastic Press Association, 1991.

Hall, Homer. *High School Journalism*. New York: Rosen Group, 1985.

Harwood, William N. *Writing and Editing School News*. Third ed.; Clark Publisher, 1990.

Ingelhart, Louis E. *Press Law and Press Freedom For High School Publications: Court Cases and Related Decisions Discussing Free Expression Guarantees and Limitations For High School Students and Journalists*. Westport, Conn.: Greenwood Press, 1986.

Julian, James L. *Practical News Assignments for Student Reporters*. Fifth ed.; Dubuque, Iowa: Wm. C. Brown, 1980.

Lain, Laurence B. *The Advertising Survival Kit*. Iowa City, Iowa: Quill and Scroll 1992.

Reddick, DeWitt C. *Journalism Exercise and Resource Book: Aids for Teaching High School Journalism*. Second ed.; Belmont, Calif.: Wadsworth, 1985.

_____. *The Mass Media and the School Newspaper*. Second ed.; Belmont, Calif.: Wadsworth, 1985.

Ross, Billy I., and Ralph A. Sellmeyer. *School Publications: The Business Side*. Branson, Mo.: MOLATX Press, 1989.

Schrank, Jeffrey. *Understanding Mass Media*. Fourth ed.; Lincolnwood, Ill.: National Textbook Company, 1991.

Savedge, Charles E. *Scholastic Yearbook Fundamentals*. Second ed.; New York: Columbia Scholastic Press Association, 1992.

Smith, Helen F., ed. *Scholastic Newspaper Fundamentals.* Second ed.; New York: Columbia Scholastic Press Association, 1989. (Includes *Scholastic Newspaper Critique.*)

_____ , ed. *Springboard to Journalism.* Fifth ed.; New York: Columbia Scholastic Press Advisers Association, 1991.

Vahl, Rod. *Effective Editorial Writing.* Iowa City, Iowa: Quill and Scroll, 1991.

Photography and Photojournalism

Davis, Philip. *The Basic Photo Book.* Dubuque, Iowa: Wm. C. Brown, 1991.

_____. *Photography.* Sixth ed.; Dubuque, Iowa: Wm. C. Brown, 1989.

Eastman Kodak Company Editors. *The New Joy of Photography.* Reading, Mass.: Addison-Wesley, 1987.

Eastman Kodak Company. *Using Filters.* (The Kodak Workshop Series) Rochester, N.Y.: Eastman Kodak, 1987.

Horton, Brian. *The Picture: An Associated Press Guide to Good News Photography.* New York: Associated Press, 1989.

Hoy, Frank P. *Photojournalism: The Visual Approach.* Englewood Cliffs, N. J.: Prentice-Hall, 1986.

Kerns, Robert L. *Photojournalism: Photography with a Purpose.* Englewood Cliffs, N.J.: Prentice-Hall, 1980.

Kobre, Kenneth. *Photographing for Newspapers and Magazines.* Boston: Focal Press, 1991.

_____. *Photojournalism: The Professionals' Approach.* Second ed.; Boston, Mass.: Focal Press, 1991.

Lewis, Greg. *Photojournalism: Content and Technique.* Dubuque, Iowa: Wm. C. Brown, 1991.

Lovell, Ronald P. et. al. *Handbook of Photography.* Second ed.; Albany, N.Y.: Delmar, 1987.

Rosen, Marvin J., and Dave Devries. *Introduction to Photography: A Self-Directing Approach.* Third ed.; Boston: Houghton Mifflin Co., 1987.

Rothstein, Arthur. *Photojournalism.* Fourth ed.; Stoneham, Mass.: Focal Press, 1984.

Stedwell, David. *Photography.* Kansas City, Mo: Walsworth Publishing Company, 1991.

Teaching Tips from Kodak Teachers! Rochester, N.Y.: Eastman Kodak Company, 1979.

Vahl, Rod. *Let's Go for Great Photos.* Iowa City, Iowa: Quill and Scroll, 1991.

Vandermeulen, Carl. *Photography for Student Publications.* Orange City, Iowa: Middleburg Press, 1980.

Reporting and Editing

Associated Press. *Associated Press Stylebook and Libel Manual.* Reading, Mass.: Addison-Wesley, 1987.

Baskette, Floyd et al. *The Art of Editing.* Fifth ed.; New York: Macmillan, 1992.

Berner, R. Thomas. *Language Skills for Journalists.* Second ed.; Boston: Houghton Mifflin, 1984.

Biagi, Shirley. *Interviews That Work: A Practical Guide for Journalists.* Second ed.; Belmont, Calif.: Wadsworth Publishing Co., 1992.

Callihan, E. L. *Grammar for Journalists.* Third ed.; Radnor, Penn.: Chilton, 1979.

Dorfman, Ron, and Harry Fuller, Jr., eds. *Reporting, Writing, Editing: The QUILL Guides to Journalism.* Chicago: Society of Professional Journalists, Sigma Delta Chi, 1982.

Fedler, Fred. *Reporting for the Print Media.* Fourth ed.; San Diego: Harcourt Brace Jovanovich, 1988.

Friedlander, E. J., and John Lee. *Feature Writing for Newspapers and Magazines.* New York: Harper & Row, 1988.

Hall, Donald. *Writing Well.* Sixth ed.; Glenview, Ill.: Scott, Foresman and Company, 1988.

Harriss, Julian, and B. Kelly Leiter. *The Complete Reporter.* Sixth ed.; New York: Macmillan, 1991.

Hughes, Helen M. *News and the Human Interest Story.* New Brunswick, N.J.: Transaction Books, 1980.

Jacobi, Peter. *Writing with Style: The News Story and the Feature.* Chicago: Lawrence Ragan Communications, 1982.

Kessler, Lauren, and Duncan McDonald. *When Words Collide: A Journalist's Guide to Grammar and Style.* Third ed.; Belmont, Calif.: Wadworth, 1992.

Maberry, D. L. *Tell Me About Yourself: How to Interview Anyone From Your Friends to Famous People.* Minneapolis: Lerner Publications, 1985.

MacDougall, Curtis D. *Interpretive Reporting.* Ninth ed.; New York: Macmillan, 1987.

McGuire, John F. *Words in Action: The 5 C's Approach to Good Writing.* Lanham, Md.: University Press of America, 1984.

Mencher, Melvin. *News Reporting and Writing.* Fifth ed.; Dubuque, Iowa: Wm. C. Brown, 1990.

_____. *Basic News Writing.* Fourth ed.; Dubuque, Iowa: Wm. C. Brown, 1992.

Metz, William. *Newswriting: From Lead to "30."* Third ed.; Englewood Cliffs, N.J.: Prentice-Hall, 1990.

Metzler, Ken. *Creative Interviewing.* Second ed.; Englewood

Cliffs, N.J.: Prentice-Hall, 1989.

———. *Newsgathering*. Second ed.; Englewood Cliffs, N.J.: Prentice-Hall, 1986.

Quill and Scroll. *Stylebook*. Iowa City, Iowa: Quill and Scroll, 1992.

The Missouri Group. *News Reporting and Writing*. Third ed.; New York, St. Martin's Press, 1988.

Stewart, Charles J. *Interviewing Principles and Practices: A Project Text*. Fourth ed.; Dubuque, Iowa: Kendall-Hunt, 1988.

Stewart, Charles J., and William B. Cash. *Interviewing: Principles and Practices*. Sixth ed.; Dubuque, Iowa: Wm. C. Brown, 1991.

Strunk, William, Jr., and E. B. White. *The Elements of Style*. Third ed.; New York: Macmillan, 1979.

Yu, Frederick T. *Get it Right; Write it Tight: The Beginning Reporter's Handbook*. Revised ed.; Honolulu: East-West Center, 1985.

Companies Offering High School Journalism Production Aids

Art Direction Book Company
10 East 39th Street
New York, NY 10016

Offers catalog of books that focus on design and layout, *Art Direction* magazine, and some clip art.

Artmaster
500 N. Claremont Blvd.
Claremont, CA 91711

Handles catalog orders for clip art packets and individual collections. Phone (714) 626-8065.

Chartpak
One River Road
Leeds, MA 01053

Handles catalog orders for clip art, borders, and art supplies. Catalogs may be obtained only through local Chartpak dealers. To find local dealers, phone (800) 882-2009 in Massachusetts; in other states, phone (800) 628-1910.

Color King
1401 East Douglas
Wichita, KS 67211

Handles catalog orders for equipment for graphic artists and painters. Catalog cost: $1. Phone (800) 835-1057 or (316) 263-8749.

Dover Publications, Inc.
31 East 2nd Street
Mineola, NY 11501

Bills itself as the "World's Largest Selection of Copyright-Free Art." Offers collections of clip art, from letters to designs.

Dynamic Graphics, Inc.
600 N. Forest Park Drive.
Peoria, IL 61614-3592

Offers monthly clip art service, print media service, thematic art packages, desktop art packages and graphics, and graphic arts bookshelf. Phone (309) 688-8800.

Educational Filmstrips
1423 19th Street
Huntsville, TX 77340

Offers filmstrips and cassettes on topics such as basic darkroom techniques, photography, and improving school newswriting.

Graphic Products Corporation
3601 Edison Place
Rolling Meadows, IL 60008

Handles catalog orders for borders, letters, and graphic arts equipment. Catalog cost: $2.95 Phone (312) 392-1476.

Greg Evans Features
660 Elm Tree Lane
San Marcos, CA 92069

Offers "Fogarty," a comic strip concerning teacher problems, and "Luann at School," a comic strip concerning student interests. Phone (619) 744-4301.

Half-Time Boosters, Inc.
P.O. Box 1749
Stone Mountain, GA 30086-1749

Handles ads for major fast-food chains and stores.

Hartco Products Company, Inc.
P. O. Box 46, Dept. 107
West Jefferson, OH 43162

Handles catalog orders for all types of supplies and equipment used in print media production. Phone (614) 879-8315 to place orders.

High School News and Graphics
c/o Tribune Media Services
64 East Concord Street.
Orlando, FL 32801

Offers bi-weekly mailing of current news items, including summaries of news that would interest students, drawing of newsmakers, and suggestions for student editors. Also sells a graphics kit. Phone (800) 322-3068, ext. 754.

New England Newspaper Supply Co.
P. O. Box 348
Millbury, MA 01527-0348

Catalog orders for all types of supplies and equipment ued in print media production. In Massachusetts, phone (800) 922-8306; in other states, phone (800) 225-7729.

Silicon Express
5955 E. Main Street
Columbus, OH 43213

Ofers computer graphics programs and newsroom programs for PCs. Phone (800) 228-0755.

Southwest Media Service
3601 N. Lincoln
Oklahoma City, OK 73105

Handles advertising for United States Army. Phone (405) 524-4421.

Stratton-Christian Press, Inc.
Box 1055
University Place Station
Des Moines, IA 50311-0055

Offers journalism posters, teaching brochures, and other aids for student publications advisers and English teachers.

Volk Clip Art
Pleasantville, NJ 08232

Offers a variety of thematic clip art packets and a monthly "Issues and Events" service. In New Jersey, phone (800) 233-7973; in other states, phone (800) 227-7048.

World Wide Photos
50 Rockefeller Plaza
New York, NY 10020

Offers packages of wire service news photos for use in student publications.